BROOKLYN
MY WORLD

**THE COMPLETELY UNAUTHORISED FURTHER MEMOIRS
OF EVERYONE'S FAVOURITE TODDLER!**

A.C. Parfitt

JOHN BLAKE

Published by John Blake Publishing Ltd,
3 Bramber Court, 2 Bramber Road,
London W14 9PB, England

First published in paperback 2001

ISBN 1903402 65 4

British Library Cataloguing-in-Publication Data:

A catalogue record for this book is
available from the British Library.

Typeset by GDAdesign

Printed in Great Britain by
Creative Print and Design (Wales),
Ebbw Vale, Gwent.

1 3 5 7 9 10 8 6 4 2

Papers used by John Blake Publishing Limited are natural,
recyclable products made from wood grown in sustainable forests.
The manufacturing processes conform to the environmental
regulations of the country of origin.

THE STORY SO FAR...

A **NOT-VERY LONG TIME** ago, on a different planet to everyone else, there lived a celebrity couple whose gorgeousness and talent were the amazement of the civilised world. Known to all men as 'Posh 'n' Becks', they were the most beautiful celebrities humankind had hitherto seen, and their haircuts became the stuff of legend. No one, it seemed, could thrust them from the rocky pinnacle of their fame.

Until, that is, the day that Posh did conceive and bring forth a son. And they called his name Brooklyn, after the place where he was conceived. And Brooklyn breathed a sigh of relief, and thanked his lucky stars that he had not been dubbed 'kitchen floor'. And he surveyed the glory of his parents' iconography, and he said to himself: 'I'll have a bit of that!'

For a long year did Brooklyn battle against the malign forces of the Big Bad Evil Ginger One; and his heart was rent asunder by the sweet affections of the glorious Baby Spice, who, as all men know, is the loveliest creature under the sun.

And Brooklyn did take up a crayon, and he commenced a diary which, over the years, would become a sought-after and important document of those heady times.

The rest, gentle reader, is history…

MARCH 2000

Sunday March 19th

AAAAAAAAAAAAAAAAAAAAAAAAAA
AAAAAAAaaaaaaaaaaaaaaaaaaaaaaaaaaaaaa
aaarrrrrrrrrrrrrrrrrrrrrrrrrrrrrrrrrrrrgggggggg
gggggggggggggggggggggggggggggggggggggggg
gghhhhhhhhhhhhhhhhhhhhhhhhhhhhhhhh
hhhhhhhhhhhhhhhhhh!!!!!!!!!!!!!!!!!!!!!!

Monday March 20th

This just can't be happening! C'mon, Mum.
C'mon, Dad. Spare me the indignity. Spare
me the humiliation.

Tuesday March 21st

OK, guys, let's be serious now. Dad, you know I respect you. You know I look up to you like, well, like a father. You know nothing you can do will make me see you as anything other than the model parent and modern-day icon that you are (with the possible exception of the sarong-in-public issue, but let's leave that for a moment, huh?). But please, please, spare me this.

As you may have guessed, dear diary, all is not well at Beckingham Palace. There I am, quietly minding my own business, doing my funky little Brooklyn-related activities (trying to get on top of the whole toddling business, practising my chat-up lines for the numerous women in my life, occasionally wetting myself – you get the picture ...) when home comes Dad with a shaved head!!!! Talk about inconsiderate – I've spent the first year of my life getting used to the idiosyncrasies of having an old man who spends more time styling his hair than working out which way round to put his trousers on (and that's really saying something, lemme tell ya), when all of a sudden he turns up looking like some kind of huge walking peanut.

But hey, I'm a man of the world, I can take such terrors in my stride. If he wants to do this kind of thing, that's hunky-dory by me. *But I've heard them plotting.* Well, if the truth be told, it hardly took any highly tuned covert operational skills to work out what they've got in mind. Mum picked me up, tweaked my nose (I *wish* she wouldn't do that), and came out with the words that strike fear into my young heart: 'Who's going to have a cutie ickle haircut like his handsome daddy, then?'

Need I say more?

Wednesday March 22nd

A year. A whole year it's taken me to establish the fine rug on my head that makes me such a wow with the chicks (along with my irresistible personality and knock-'em-dead smile, of course). And it hasn't been easy, I can tell you. When I first arrived on the scene I was bald as a coot – a severe disability for a junior Casanova like me. I'll never forget the first time Baby Spice had the, frankly, quite appalling lack of tact to mention it:

> **Baby Spice:** *Who's a cute little baldy, then?*
> **Brooklyn:** *Hey, sweetheart, haven't you heard? Baldness is a sign of buckets of testosterone. It's a manifestation of my virility …*

OK, so I handled it pretty well, but you

see my problem. Then, after a while, joy, rapture! A few follicles start to sprout, and over the next few months I develop the splendid head of hair I'm sporting now. But not for much longer it seems …

Thursday March 23rd

We go to the hairdressers on Saturday. My doom awaits.

Despite my paranoia, I've noticed that Mum seems to be incredibly keen on Dad's new look – she can't keep her hands off him. I'm not reading too much into it, though. It may be that a shaved head increases a dude's sex-appeal, but let's not forget that Mum thought Dad looked cool in a skirt. I can't take it as read that her taste is entirely representative of the rest of womankind …

Friday March 24th

One day to go.

You know, it wouldn't be so bad if it weren't for my sneaking suspicion that Dad only asked for 'a number two all over' because he can't count any higher.

Saturday March 25th

As I write, I await our trip to the hair executioner. Soon I will be shorn of my flowing locks, and who knows what kind of irreparable damage it will do to my cheeky good looks? I only hope that it doesn't harm my chances with the women in my life: the fragrant Baby Spice and Mrs Madonna's daughter, the lovely Lourdes. I'd be the first to admit that my relationship with them both has been blowing a bit hot and cold, but I'd hate to think that their adoration of me should be at all diminished because of a paltry haircut.

Still, I must learn to be philosophical. Disasters like this are all part of the rich tapestry of life, especially with a Mum and Dad like mine …

Sunday March 26th

Too traumatised even to consider writing anything …

Monday March 27th

Maybe it was all a horrible dream. Maybe if I pinch myself hard enough I'll wake up.

Tuesday March 28th

Ouch!

Wednesday March 29th

Nope. It wasn't a horrible dream, it was a horrible reality. (The nightmare I had about Mum starting to purchase my togs from Top Shop instead of Emporio Armani – now *that* was a horrible dream …)

I suppose I should look on the bright side,

though. Having witnessed my first Beckham family outing to the hairdresser, I do feel I've had a truly eye-opening experience that is granted to only a select few. The hairdresser seemed nice enough, although he did seem very pleased to see Dad – suspiciously so, if you ask me. He sat him down in the chair, stroked his scalp (ugh!) and said, 'So what can we do for you today, luvvie?'

Dad looked a bit confused and muttered, 'Erm, I think it was a number … um, hang on, Victoria did tell me,' at which point Mum steamed in and gave her instructions. Dad looked much happier, bless him.

The less said about my stint of tonsure torture the better. Suffice to say that I emerged looking rather more follically challenged than when I went in. This haircut's taken years off me. Well, one year to be precise – I look like a babe in arms.

Thursday March 30th

I'm very glad I don't seem to be displaying Dad's worrying tendency to grow this funny furry face fungus. Dad's beard is longer than his hair at the moment. He really should do something about it – he looks like he's put his head on upside down …

Friday March 31st

Scary Spice is coming round with her daughter Phoenix Chi tomorrow. I hope she handles my recent predicament with tact and sensitivity. I think I'm safe enough – she's pretty sassy, and she generally knows how to behave.

   On second thoughts, she'll probably laugh her head off.

APRIL
2000

Saturday April 1st

Well, it was touch and go:

> **Phoenix Chi**: *OK, dude, give it to me straight. It's some kinda April Fool, right?*
> **Brooklyn**: *Don't flatter yourself, sweetheart. OK, so I like to amuse you, but do you really think I'd go to these kind of lengths?*
> **Phoenix**: *From where I'm toddling, you ain't got any kinda lengths. So what's the story? Did you see the Big Bad Evil*

Ginger One and have all your hair fall out in fright?

Brooklyn*: Very funny, Phoenix Chi. Actually, er, this is the latest style. All the cats are going for this kind of look now. My dad's a bit of a trend-setter, in case you hadn't noticed.*

Phoenix*: Actually, I hadn't noticed many guys dressing up in skirts and putting hankies on their heads, no. But hey, I'll take yo' word for it. If my pal Brooklyn says bald is in, then bald is in.*

Brooklyn*: You should try it yourself.*

Phoenix: No way, José. I'm waitin' till my hair's long enough for dreads ...

I dunno what dreads are, but I felt too shy to ask. Phoenix Chi can be pretty unforgiving about stuff like that.

Sunday April 2nd

I couldn't help noticing that Phoenix Chi is getting quite proficient in the old adult-speak department these days. She's a bit older than I am, so I'm not too concerned that she's ahead of me, but it would be nice to be able to start conversing with Mum and Dad on a more meaningful level. (It's gonna take a bit of input from Dad, I know, but I'm willing to encourage him.)

Monday April 3rd

At the moment I can manage 'Goo!' and, occasionally, 'Ga!'. Don't get me wrong – I get reactions from the Oldies that melt even my stony heart when I say these words – but I do feel the need for a more versatile repertoire …

Tuesday April 4th

BROOKLYN'S LIST OF USEFUL PHRASES TO PRACTISE

'Feed me, baby!'

(On second thoughts, make that 'A large T-Bone steak, please.' OK, so it's a bit premature teeth-wise, but I'm hugely going off the nonsense that Mum's been serving up: mushy peas, mushy carrots, mushy this, mushy that, mushy the other. I need something a bit more manly and substantial!)

'How many times do I have to tell you, I don't wear anything without a label?'

(I'll say one thing for Mum and Dad – that's not a phrase I can envisage myself using with them very often. But it'll come in useful with anyone else who has plans to buy me gear that is, how can I put it, not quite befitting my superstar status …)

'Hey Baby/Lourdes (delete as appropriate), you're looking kinda foxy. How about a cosy evening in, just the two of us?'

(OK, call me fickle, but I've been through the mill as far as affairs of the heart are concerned, what with Baby Spice toying with my affections and Lourdes playing hard-to-get. A toddler's gotta do what a toddler's gotta do, and if that means playing one off against the other, then so be it.)

'Begone, Evil Ginger One. I cast ye out!'

(Sounds dramatic, I know, but I need to be able to stand up against the malign forces of the evil Ginger Spice. Mum and Dad would be no good – they turn into gibbering wrecks every time her name is mentioned ...)

And that's just for starters. I'd better get practising.

Wednesday April 5th

Hmmmm ... maybe I'm being a little too

optimistic. I spent the day shopping with Dad, and I was desperate to say, 'I'll have the *red* Calvin Klein puffa jacket.' Unfortunately, all that came out was 'Goo!', followed by a sort of gurgling noise and a bit of a dribble – and that was only Dad! What was worse, he couldn't make out what I was saying either. And even worse than that, he bought me the *green* jacket. He *knows* green isn't my colour. If he thinks I'm wearing it, he's got another thing coming …

Thursday April 6th

This is getting daft. I've got to find some way of communicating with Mum and Dad. If I could only tell them what I'm thinking, the whole haircut fiasco could have been avoided, and I'd be the proud owner of a natty little red puffa jacket …

I'm gonna have to swallow my pride and ask Phoenix Chi how she goes about it. She's coming round tomorrow …

Friday April 7th

Well, I picked up a few pointers.

Brooklyn: *Hey, sweetheart, you've gotta help me with this adult-talk business.*
Phoenix: *Don't sweetheart me, dude. You gotta learn some respect …*
Brooklyn: *Calm down, calm down. C'mon, gimme the low-down. What've I got to do?*
Phoenix: *Practise, dude. Practise, practise, practise. Hit on a phrase, and stick with it. It'll come pretty soon.*
Brooklyn: *What was your first phrase?*
Phoenix: *Never mind, it ain't important.*

Ha! I happen to know for a fact that her first word was 'Mama' – despite her ice-cool exterior, I bet her first phrase was something similarly unremarkable. As long as my first words are reasonably hip, I reckon I'll be able to outshine her.

Saturday April 8th

BROOKLYN'S LIST OF EMBARRASSING
FIRST PHRASES – TO BE AVOIDED.

'Brooklyn go potty.' (No comment – the humiliation would be insufferable.)

'Daddy go potty.' (Meaningless – Daddy went potty ages ago…)

Let's face it, anything to do with potties is out.

Sunday April 9th

I'm going to have to practise something zappy, something hip – something that says Brooklyn's arrived and he's here to stay …

Monday April 10th

'Ladies and gentleman, big it up for Baby

Brooklyn.' I like it! It's not too ambitious, but it has pizzazz, it has definition. I'd better get practising …

Tuesday April 11th

'Ladies and gentlemen, big it up for Baby Brooklyn! Ladies and gentlemen, big it up for Baby Brooklyn! Ladies and gentlemen, big it up …'

Wednesday April 12th

' … for Baby Brooklyn.' Gotta keep at it. It's hard work, but you know what they say – no pain, no gain …

Thursday April 13th

Oh dear. I'm beginning to feel a bit disheartened. This speaking business is much harder than it looks. Every time I try to say something, it comes out as a series of coos. I sound like a bleedin' jackdaw.

Perhaps I should just resign myself to life as a mute.

Friday April 14th

I'm beginning to wonder if my inability to express myself is some kind of hereditary disorder. Mum asked Dad today if he'd remembered to clean his football boots, and he just looked a bit blank and didn't say anything. Mum looked at him and said, 'Well did you?' and Dad just said 'Um …' An admirable example of scintillating rhetoric it was not!

You know, Mum and Dad are very sweet, but I do sometimes worry about my gene pool …

Saturday April 15th

Have just had the most shocking news. Am too confused and bemused to write about it. I'll fill you in tomorrow.

Sunday April 16th

Jeepers creepers! This, my dear diary, you will not believe.

Now I don't want anyone to think that I don't reckon my Dad's talented. I'm the first to sing his praises – he can certainly kick a ball, that much is certain. And he can shop. Boy oh boy can he shop. If shopping were a sport, he'd be Premier Division.

Yep, the lad has talent, you can't deny that. But why oh why oh why can't he accept his limitations? I can just about toddle, but you don't see me running marathons. I can utter a couple of sounds, but you don't see me reciting obscure poetry. Why can't Dad follow my example? Why can't he just stick to what he's good at?

And what exactly is his hare-brained scheme (or should I say no-hair-brained scheme)? He's going to write a book! I'm speechless (OK, OK, so I'm speechless anyway, but you take my point ...) This can only end in disaster.

It's Mum's birthday tomorrow. Ordinarily I'd be excited, but I'm afraid the shock of this recent intelligence is having an unpredictable effect on me ...

Monday April 17th

Happy Birthday Mum! Actually, it's been quite an understated day, in comparison to the usual Beckham birthday – Dad bought Mum a few grand's worth of jewels, of course, but that's rather par for the course these days. After all, what do you get the woman who has everything? (Actually, a few singing lessons wouldn't go amiss, but I can see why Dad didn't go down that route – I'm not sure she'd have taken it that well ...)

Dad very sweetly gave Mum a lovely card, though. It said: 'Deer viktorya, Happy birfday, love ~~Daved~~ ~~dayvid~~ Becks xxx'. Mum seemed very touched. 'Oh David,' she practically fluttered, 'did you write that all by yourself?' Dad was proud as a peacock.

Of course, herein lies the nub of the problem regarding Dad's latest venture. You do realise that he's going to have to learn to write before he can embark upon this misguided project. I just hope he doesn't start nicking my crayons again …

Tuesday April 18th

… and I wish Mum wouldn't encourage him. Dad's been looking a bit nervous about the whole affair, and rightly so. She sat him down and said, 'Don't worry, David, it's going to be brilliant. We'll just make sure there's plenty of pictures in it, shall we?'

Wednesday April 19th

Actually, the picture idea isn't a bad one, just as long as they don't put anything embarrassing in. Good old Mum – sometimes she does have her head screwed on right.

Thursday April 20th

The more I think about the picture plan, the more I like it. It'll be a good opportunity for me to present myself to the world in a slightly funkier guise than I've hitherto been able to. I still haven't forgotten the pictures of Mum and Dad's wedding that they showed the world, with me resplendent in a purple dress. (Purple! A dress! The scars still haven't healed.) Just so long as they keep a sense of proportion, I could come out of the whole thing pretty well.

But don't let this make you believe that I approve of the whole venture. Know your limits, Dad! You don't see *me* trying to write a book, now do you?

Friday April 21st

Actually, that's not such a bad idea. My own book! What stories I could tell. Of course, I'd have to edit things down a bit to put Mum and Dad in a slightly more favourable light, but I don't reckon that's beyond me. Just so long as nobody gets hold of my secret diaries – some things are meant for my eyes only.

Saturday April 22nd

Eek! Mum's been at the piano again. I think Dad's been regretting buying it for her as a Christmas present ever since she laid eyes on it. I've been giving some pretty hefty thought to having a good old crying session, but I don't think I can really bear to put Dad through the strain. He's been wandering round the house looking a bit the worse for wear, and it's hardly surprising – if either of us had any hair we'd both be pulling it out by now.

It's not just Mum's musical prowess (or lack of it) that's putting so much stress on the old man. Reading between the lines (something Dad would have difficulty doing, I think) I can tell he's worried about this book thing. I know he brought it upon himself, but you gotta feel sorry for the poor guy – he has enough trouble writing the shopping list, let alone a fully fledged work of autobiography.

I think I'll give them a break from the old crying for a bit …

Sunday April 23rd

And anyway, I'm getting a bit too old for

crying. I have plenty of ulterior motives for acting with a little more dignity now that I'm on the brink of toddlerhood:

BROOKLYN'S REASONS
TO BE CHEERFUL

1. The ladies. *I know I go on about this, but the one thing I've learned in my short life is that without luurve,* je ne suis rien. *I have to get my on/off relationship with Baby Spice back on track (Baby Spice and Spice Baby – it's a match made in heaven) and I happen to know that my cheeky little smile makes her weak at the knees – she's only human, after all.*

2. Mum and Dad. *There are plenty of things I need from them (decent grub, designer gear, a particularly swish little pair of Nikes I saw when I was out shopping with Dad the other day …). I've noticed that generally they are more*

receptive to my needs when I'm being nice.
3. The Big Bad Evil Ginger One. *Although I've managed to foil her attempts at world domination in the past, it's important that I don't get complacent. I'm constantly on the lookout for signs of danger, but I know that fear is her most powerful weapon. A constant smile on my face is bound to wrong-foot her.*

Yep, a happy little chappie I'm gonna be.

Monday April 24th

Well, I'm smiling. Mum's still playing the bleedin' piano, but I'm still smiling. This is what you call dedication …

Tuesday April 25th

Football practice with Dad tomorrow. It'll be a blessed release on the old lugholes, that's for sure. Dad asked Mum if she thought she'd done enough piano playing today, and she went a bit nutty. Her exact words were: 'David, don't you understand my need to express myself through my art? Can't you see that, just as Wordsworth had his poetry, Cezanne had his painting and Rodin had his sculpture, I have my [at this point she put her forehead in her hand and furrowed her brow] *my music.*' And she flounced out of the room, tossing her hair (I wish I could do that – huh! chance would be a fine thing), muttering something about the creative urges that burn within her.

Poor old Dad looked a bit confused by the whole affair. He sat at the piano and played 'Chopsticks'. Between you and me, dear diary, whilst it was hardly the apotheosis of twenty-first-century musical achievement, after Mum's attempts it was music to my ears.

Wednesday April 26th

Wahey! Football with Dad. It was the first time I'd been let loose on the pitch since I've learned to put one foot in front of the other. I'll concede that I haven't quite developed Dad's inimitable footballing style yet, but I don't reckon I'm far off. I kicked, I dribbled, I crossed, I, er, I fell over quite a bit (look, I'm a beginner at this walking thang, OK?); all in all, I cut a dash. Wembley, here I come …

Dad made the mistake, though, of mentioning his book plans to some of his team-mates. A rather ominous silence descended on them when he did that, which doesn't bode well. Half of them are one player short of a football team, if you know what I mean, and even *they* think it's a bad idea. Dad seemed oblivious to it all, though. I wish he'd take note.

Thursday April 27th

It's Dad's birthday on Tuesday. I happen to have overheard Mum saying she's going to buy him a nice pen as one of his presents. Hmmmm ...

Friday April 28th

I can't help thinking that they have a habit of buying each other entirely inappropriate gifts. Let's look at the facts. Dad buys Mum a piano, when it's entirely clear to all and sundry that something by Cartier or Tiffany – both of whom specialise in gifts that are essentially SILENT!!!! – would have been far more the thing. And Mum buys Dad a pen. Need I explain the problems with that one?

Saturday April 29th

Spent most of the day playing peek-a-boo

with Dad. To be honest, it's not a pastime I'm wild about, but the old boy seems to love it. In fact, he wanted to play it with Mum, but she gave him a bit of a withering look so he had to settle for yours truly. I'm proud to report that I had him for breakfast. I don't want to sound competitive or anything – after all, I'm the first to admit he's got the edge over me on the football pitch – but when it comes to peek-a-boo, nobody can touch Brooklyn.

Of course, it does help that Dad forgets what he's supposed to say. Some might say that that gives me an unfair advantage, but I don't think so – rules, after all, are rules.

I almost managed to say the words 'peek-a-boo' myself, actually, but fortunately they came out as 'Ga, wrrrssstff, coooo …' Thank God for that, huh? Imagine the shame of breaking my silence with something so childish …

Sunday April 30th

I knew it! I bleedin' knew it! The blighter's got his eyes on my crayons again! There I was, happily sketching away (while we're on the subject, I can't help feeling there's something Picasso-esque about my artistic output ...), when he comes along, nicks one of the crayons and starts trying to sign his name. If I could only speak, I'd tell him that David Beckham isn't spelt 'X' – it would make such a difference to his life.

You'll be pleased to know that I managed to keep on smiling, as per my resolution, but it was tough. Boy, it was tough.

MAY
2000

Monday May 1st

Dad's birthday tomorrow. I'm having second thoughts about the pen gift. Maybe it's not such a bad idea – at least it'll keep his grubby little mitts off my crayons …

Tuesday May 2nd

Oh, what a disaster. Poor old Dad, he means well, I know he does, but he just can't help getting it wrong. Mum gave him the pen (Cartier, solid gold, couldn't have cost less than ten big ones) over breakfast,

44

and he smiled a bit unconvincingly. 'You do know what it is, don't you David?' Mum asked him.

'Erm, course I do,' Dad simpered, but I could tell he was lying. Sure enough, a couple of hours later, Mum found him throwing it at his Alex Ferguson dartboard. She went ballistic – 'It's a pen, David, to help you write your book – not a dart!' Personally, I don't know why she was so cross – Dad got a wicked bull's-eye; it's clearly a nifty piece of kit.

So Mum sulked for a bit, but Dad cheered her up by dressing up in one of her thongs and dancing round the kitchen. Quite why Mum encourages him in this sort of behaviour is absolutely beyond me – if I thought anyone knew what they were up to I'd never be able to show my face in public again. Anyway, Mum told Dad she'd sing him a special song. Dad was very good – he didn't grimace even a little bit. And he'd obviously taken on board what she said about her need to express herself artistically. He said, 'Erm, what I find most moving in your work is your creative use of dissonance, your ability to fuse the atonal with the modern mainstream, to challenge people's perceptions of what can and can't be music …'

Personally I was knocked out when Dad said that – it's the first time I've ever heard him use words of more than two syllables. Mum didn't seem to take it that way, though. 'I was singing "Happy Birthday", actually David,' she said, before storming out.

Ooops.

Wednesday May 3rd

Oh dear. Mum's sulking. Actually, Dad doesn't look too upset. At least it keeps her away from the piano …

Dad's got a big match at Old Trafford on Saturday, and apparently I get to go along. Mum's been talking about dressing me up in a Manchester United football strip for the occasion, so it seems I'm going to be on display to all and sundry. I'm not quite sure how I feel about this – if I'm going to be on public view I think I'd much prefer to be wearing something a little more recherché. A mixture of silks and satins, I think. Prada would be appropriate, perhaps a little Dior. I can't deny I'm feeling a bit nervous about the whole thing – Mum does have an unnerving habit of bunging me in the most embarrassing gear she can find when she knows I'm gonna be on public view.

Thursday May 4th

Hmmm … It's all going to be on telly, too – everyone's going to be watching: Baby Spice, Phoenix Chi, even Lourdes (although she is a bit posh to watch the footy). Mum, I'd better look funky …

Friday May 5th

D-day tomorrow. Can't help feeling a bit nervous. Ah well, the adrenaline will help my performance.

It's just struck me – we'd better win. D'ya hear that, Dad? If you reckon I'm gonna be there to represent the losing side, you got another thing coming!

Saturday May 6th

Lumme, what a day. Far too exhausted to write much – will fill you in tomorrow.

Sunday May 7th

I'm a superstar! My public loves me!

Actually, if I'm being honest, we had a pretty iffy start to the day. Mum chucked me in this Man U kit, which would be OK in itself if it weren't for the fact that she made me wear these stupid football boots that say 'Daddy' on them. Now, perhaps I'm being dense, but I fail to see the logic here. Dad gets rid of his shoes, which very helpfully had the words 'Left' and 'Right' written on them, in favour of a pair that say 'Brooklyn'. Not only does this mean it takes him twice as long to put his shoes on (i.e. two hours – he still hasn't got the hang of those laces), it also makes him look bleedin' ridiculous.

So then, I get a pair that say 'Daddy'. Why? Now, an exclusive pair of designer boots that say 'Brooklyn' on them, I could live with. They'd have panache, they'd have cachet. They'd signify my individuality, they'd show the chicks that I'm my own man. As it is, I look like, well, like a daddy's boy. And to be fair, the 'Daddy' label would be much more useful for my old man –

they'd remind him that he is Daddy, and not Mummy, as his occasional cross-dressing antics would seem to suggest he thinks he might be.

So the day started badly, but fair's fair – it went uphill from there, all thanks to my old man. Not only did they win, but he scored a goal! How the crowd ooohhed! How the crowd aaahhed! And then yours truly went out on the pitch. How the crowd ooohhed! How the crowd aaahhed! How the crowd ooohhed again, this time in a slightly gooier way, a reaction that Dad, I'm afraid, simply can't milk out of them. Clearly my inherent style, charm and charisma shone through the slightly duff gear I was sporting – they couldn't get enough of me!

Dad's goal meant that his team won something called the Premiership – I don't know what that is, and frankly I'm not too fussed. The football was, I'm afraid, secondary to the spectacle of Baby Brooklyn taking to the field. I hope Baby Spice saw the whole thing – her knees will have turned to jelly …

Monday May 8th

Mum seems to have forgiven Dad for his birthday antics, as he's started practising with his new pen – it took him a bit of time to work out which was the business end, but he's just about got the hang of it, I think.

So that's the good news. The bad news is, I've heard them having a very worrying conversation. They were discussing Dad's forthcoming foray into the world of literature, and he was, understandably getting a bit nervous. So Mum said, 'Come on David. If the Big Bad Evil Ginger One can write a book, then so can you.'

I wish she'd engage brain before opening mouth. As soon as she mentioned the name of the Evil Ginger One, she seemed to realise what a terrible thing she'd done. A distinct gloom fell upon the room, and the sun went behind a cloud, casting a frosty atmosphere all around. The wind started to howl, and I'm sure I saw an evil-looking raven fly past the window. Mum came and picked me up, and wrapped her arms protectively around me, before continuing in a much more subdued voice, 'So come on, David. What letter does your name begin with?' But they seemed to have lost their appetite for scholarship, and spent the rest of the day moping around. Even a game of peek-a-boo couldn't cheer Dad up.

I had no idea that the Big Bad Evil Ginger One had written a book. It must be a terrifying, evil document, malevolently produced to spread her foul ideology across the world. I must consult with Phoenix Chi at the earliest available opportunity. She is the only person I know who is aware of the extent to which the Ginger One has filtered through every echelon of our society ...

Tuesday May 9th

Spent all night worrying about the Ginger One's evil gospels. I can't believe I have remained innocent of her actions for so long. Fortunately I'm seeing Phoenix Chi tomorrow. Hopefully we'll come up with something together ...

Wednesday May 10th

I don't think I was overreacting – Phoenix Chi seems as shocked as me ...

> **Brooklyn**: *Hey Phoenix Chi, terrible things are afoot.*
> **Phoenix**: *You don't have to tell me that, dude. I'm only too well aware of it ...*
> **Brooklyn**: *You are?*

Phoenix: *You said it, my friend. My mum's thinking of releasing a solo album.*

Brooklyn: *Well, OK, that's scary enough in itself …*

Phoenix: *Watch it, pal …*

Brooklyn: *Hey, hear me out, hear me out. Look, I'm going to have to fill you in with a bit of background, but you gotta promise not to laugh, OK?*

Phoenix: *I ain't making no promises I can't keep, man. Spit it out.*

Brooklyn: *Well, OK. [Very quietly]* My Dad's writing a book.

Phoenix: *Huh? Speak up, dude!*

Brooklyn: *[A bit louder]* My Dad's writing a book.

Phoenix: *What's that? Your Dad's always getting booked? Well, tell me something I don't know, kiddio …*

Brooklyn: *Ok! Ok! My Dad's writing a book.*

Have I got to spell it out for you?

Phoenix: *[Stunned silence]*

Brooklyn: *Well, c'mon, say something.*

Phoenix: *[More stunned silence]*

Brooklyn: *OK, so now I've got your attention, I can fill you in. I heard the Oldies talking about it, and my mum said that if the Big Bad Evil Ginger One can write a book, then so can Dad.*

Phoenix: *[Gasp!]*

Brooklyn: *So like I said, terrible things are afoot.*

Phoenix: *You said it, dude. The implications are colossal. This means that the Ginger One must have a following. She's got disciples, and this disgusting work must be their bible. I'm gonna have to get my people onto this …*

Thursday May 11th

I'm not quite sure how I feel about Phoenix Chi's reaction yesterday. On the one hand, I'm relieved to have a soul mate (and one thing I've gotta say for PC – she's sure got soul …) with whom I can share this terrifying intelligence. But on the other hand I was expecting a less extreme reaction – she's normally pretty unflappable: the fact that she's as worried as I am is a real cause for concern.

Friday May 12th

Suddenly I see the world in a different light. Everywhere I look, I see the potential for evil. Everyone I see, I see as a possible disciple of the Evil One. How many of them have read her foul book? Something is rotten in the state of England …

Saturday May 13th

Way to go! We're off on holiday on Tuesday – the good ol' US of A. It'll be a good opportunity to see if the Evil One's influence has spread across the water. America should breathe a sigh of relief that I'm on my way. I see myself as a secret agent, bravely battling against the inevitable tide of darkness that could soon be upon us. Plus, we should get the opportunity to pick up some natty designer labels ... that way, everyone wins!

Sunday May 14th

I shan't be taking my diary with me on hols. It's too dangerous. I know it will be safe tucked up at home – abroad, who knows what agents of the enemy will be able to get their hands on it? Vigilance is the key!

Monday May 15th

Spent the day packing. What an operation – you'd think we were going for a year, not a week. Mum packed everything bar the kitchen sink, and that was only because she wanted to dissuade Dad from practising his tap dancing. We leave first thing in the morning – see you in a week!

Tuesday May 16th

Wednesday May 17th

Thursday May 18th

Friday May 19th

Saturday May 20th

Sunday May 21st

Monday May 22nd

Tuesday May 23rd

Phew, it's nice to be back in Blighty, but I must say I've got a bit of a taste for the old West Coast. LA – land of opportunity. The sun, the sea, the girls … yep, it's my kinda town.

The highlight of the trip was a visit to Disneyland – loads of fun, and a good way to get my mind off my worries. I particularly like hanging around with the dudes in the silly clothes and funny hats – but enough about Mum and Dad; Mickey and Goofy were quite a laugh too.

And the shopping! Oh, the shopping! When Mum and Dad hit the stores together, there's really no stopping them. I've gotta give them their due – they share my love of fine things. You can see where I get my 'love of shopping' genes from. And my love of shopping for jeans (Armani only, if you please).

The only downside of the whole trip was

the tuck. Don't get me wrong – it looked great, and our American cousins sure know how to eat – but unfortunately Mum is still pummelling the globs of dodgy-looking mashed stuff down my gullet. It's incredibly insensitive of them to feed me on this rubbish and then go and gorge themselves on big tasty-looking burgers. Still, it kept Dad happy – normally if he goes a whole day without one of his favourite Jammie Dodgers, he becomes insufferable. Across the pond, he didn't have one for a whole week, and we didn't hear a peep out of him.

Wednesday May 24th

You'll be relieved to hear, dear diary, that I didn't notice any signs of the Evil Ginger One having infiltrated the American continent; but I'm not going to cease my vigilance. I know Mum and Dad will have gone out of their way to shelter me from any evidence of her existence, which is all very well, but it doesn't help me on my crusade.

Thursday May 25th

A-ha! The lovely Baby Spice comes round tomorrow. It's been some months since I've seen her, and I'm feeling confident that my recent experiences have given me a groovy kind of demeanour that will set her little heart a-flutter. After all, she can't have many beaux that have been cheered by an ecstatic crowd at Old Trafford and seen through the plans of the most evil force in the world. My hair's grown a bit, too, which means I look less like a boiled egg. And since I last saw her, my ability to walk has increased tenfold – I'll be able to, quite literally, give her the run around …

Friday May 26th

Far too besotted even to consider writing.

Saturday May 27th

Aaahhh!!! Baby Spice!!!! The months have not been unkind to your gentle, alabaster features. Can you forgive me for my coolness towards you? Can you forget my fickleness?

As you may have guessed, dear diary, yesterday's meeting with the luscious Baby went very, very well:

> **Baby Spice**: *Hello little Brooklyny-wooklyny. Who hasn't seen his Aunty Emma for ages and ages and ages?*
> **Spice Baby**: *Hey sweetheart, cut the Brooklyn-wooklyny mumbo jumbo. It's time you started treating me as what I am – all man. And less of the 'Aunty'. We*

don't want any impediment to our *luuurve*, now do we?

Baby Spice*: Is your daddy going to be a famous author as well as a famous footballer?*

Spice Baby*: C'mon, babe, less of him, more of us. Did ya catch the appearance I put in at Old Trafford? Did ya see the reaction? Pretty sensational, huh? Well, if you're lucky, you can have a piece of that. C'mon, give us a kiss …*

And she did just that – a full smackeroonie right on the lips, followed by an affectionate little bout of nose rubbing.

My heart is lost to her – I can think of nothing else …

Sunday May 28th

Even the threat of the Big Bad Evil Ginger One has paled into insignificance against my re-found love of that gorgeous creature. PC will give me a hard time, I know, but that's her problem. Sometimes she can be a bit too stony-faced about affairs of the heart; she's gotta learn to relax …

Monday May 29th

When you have love in your heart, suddenly the world is a better place. I see everything in a different light – Mum's piano playing is suddenly a thing of idiosyncratic beauty; Dad went out to a party last night wearing an earring and a hanky on his head, and I even felt moderately well disposed towards him.

Tuesday May 30th

Moderately well disposed, you understand – not entirely. I may be in love, but I'm not ga-ga.

Wednesday May 31st

I see now that I have been blasé about the affections of my love. I shall make it my life's work to win her heart. Once more, she will be mine ...

JUNE
2000

Thursday June 1st

Dad spent all day at footy practice today; which gave me a bit of quality time with Mum – not that I don't class time with Dad as quality time, you understand, but it's important for me to nurture the crucial mother-baby relationship. What I really wanted to do was pick her brains about my tempestuous relationship with Baby Spice, but as you can imagine, my inability to speak slightly got in the way.

Friday June 2nd

You know, I'm definitely on the brink. I can feel myself almost forming words: it's only a matter of time before one of them pops out. How I pray it's something hip – maybe 'Big it up for Baby Brooklyn' is ambitious, but a kid's gotta aim high.

Saturday June 3rd

Dad out at footy again today. Mum refused to wash his muddy kit when he got back, so he had to try and use the washing machine by himself. This was not, as you can imagine, an unqualified success – the sooner he learns the difference between the washing machine and the oven the better, if you ask me. You can't begin to imagine how smelly a charred Man United shirt can be; and Mum had a right old whinge when Dad served up Soggy Sausages à la Washing

Powder for tea.

Personally, I think she was overreacting a bit – I'd give my right arm for a spot of Soggy Sausage. If she'd been on the constant diet of mush that I've had to put up with, she'd have considered it gourmet stuff ...

Sunday June 4th

Oh God, I'm so close! Tried a few phrases, and whilst they didn't come out exactly as I wanted, at least I'm making sounds that are a bit more manly:

What Brooklyn Tried To Say	How It Came Out
Big it up for Baby Brooklyn	Brrr!!!!
Yo Mama, Brooklyn in da House	Brrrr!!!!!

> My love is like a
> melody,
> That's sweetly
> played in tune ...   Fbluerk!!!

OK, so there's progress to be made, but I'm on the right path ...

Monday June 5th

Gimme strength! Mum could learn a thing or two about melodies sweetly played in tune, it's true; but now Dad's decided he's going to get into rap music. So at one end of the house I've got her torturing her vocal cords, and at the other I've got MC Becks trying to be Eminem. I just pray he keeps away from the dungarees ...

Tuesday June 6th

Dad out at footy again today, thank the Lord. Quite why he's chosen a musical vehicle that requires a subtle and sophisticated knowledge of the rhyme and rhythm of language, I really don't know – he has enough trouble remembering the lyrics to 'Baa Baa Black Sheep'.

Ah well, he's got a big football tournament coming up in the next few days, so that should keep his mind off such nonsense. It's called the European Cup; quite why he thinks it's so important I don't know, as he seems to have quite enough cups from where I'm standing – the kitchen's full of 'em. Still, whatever keeps him happy …

Wednesday June 7th

Yabbadabbadoo!!!!! I've done it! My first word!

Excuse my excitement, dear diary, but as you can imagine this is a pretty significant moment in my tender young life. It came from a pretty inauspicious start, I'll admit. Dad was at football practice (again!) when I was having a little chat with Mum – or rather, she was chatting and I was gurgling in my devastatingly charming way. All of a sudden, she comes out with what has to be the most terrible idea she's ever had – and that comes up against some pretty stiff competition, I can assure you. What was her gem of wisdom? Only that we should make our way down to something called a parent and toddler group!

Can you imagine anything worse? This is Brooklyn Beckham you're talking about, Mum. You can't expect me to hang out with the riffraff. What if some horrible little toddler spills gunk on my designer togs? Worse still, what if Dad takes me along dressed in a skirt? Imagine the humiliation – clearly I'd be victimised, scarred for life, rendered unable to live my life as an ordinary, well-adjusted human being. No, no, no, no, no, no, no!

And in fact that's exactly what I said: 'No!' Then I said it again for good measure. Then I said 'Brrrr' and giggled, but that was an accident. Mum didn't seem to fully appreciate the seriousness of my utterance, however – she looked quite delighted and started going all gooey. 'Just you wait till I tell your daddy!' she said, which I thought was a bit unkind – I don't want him to be jealous of my new-found ability.

Thursday June 8th

Spent all day practising my new word. Mum and Dad can't get enough of it – they go all misty eyed every time I speak. I have a powerful weapon under my belt …

Friday June 9th

'NO NO NO NO NO NO NO!' Heh heh – stand back Shakespeare.

Saturday June 10th

Can't tell you how pleased I am with my vocabulary. One of my major worries has always been that my first word would be 'nappy' or something similarly undistinguished. Now I can hold my head high with pride. And I've got confidence too – I'll be writing a book before you know it.

Which reminds me, Dad had better muscle down – the lad's got a lot to learn before he can put pen to paper …

Sunday June 11th

Hmmm … Maybe I'm getting a bit big for my booties. It's all very well saying 'No!' at every available opportunity, and it *can* be a distinct advantage having it as my only word. For example:

Mum: *Would ickle Brooklyn like Mummy to sing him a lovely lullaby?*

Brooklyn: *No!* (Actually, what I wanted to say was 'No way, José – frankly I'd rather listen to someone scraping a fork down the blackboard.' But failing that, 'No' was an acceptable alternative.)

Or:

Dad: *Would you like Daddy to give you a little kiss?*

Brooklyn: *No, no, no!* (Dad! Stubble burn – when ya gonna learn? And even if your face was as smooth as a baby's bottom (and that's smooth – trust me, I know about these things) I really don't want to get into the whole two-guys-kissing-in-public issue. *Comprende?*)

However, it has its downsides:

Mum: *Would Brooklyn like to go and see his Daddy playing football tomorrow night?*

Brooklyn: *No!* (Doh!!! Of course I wanna go – I'm the star of the show at these gigs. I've really got to raise my profile if I'm gonna get anywhere with Baby Spice …)

So as you can see, I'm really going to have to work on a bit more lingo – 'Yes!' would open up my options quite nicely, I think.

Monday June 12th

Dad's a bit nervous about tonight's game, bless him. It's a bit of a biggie – England's first game of the European Championship. Still, it's only against Portugal – they could put Mum in goal and still win, I reckon.

We're watching it on telly, worst luck.

Tuesday June 13th

Oh the indignity! Oh the humiliation! Portugal 3, England 2. Dad didn't even score a goal. What's the point of having a high-profile dad if he can't even get one in the back of the net when he's on the international stage? And against Portugal. Portugal!

Wednesday June 14th
We're playing Germany next. This is serious. Dad had better pull his socks up.

Thursday June 15th
Come to think of it, I'd be happy if he just remembered not to put his socks on inside-out. In my position, you've got to be grateful for small mercies.

Friday June 16th
One day till the Germany game. Dad's been practising all day in the garden. Fair play to him, he's managed to keep possession from the garden gnomes most of the time, but I

can't help thinking that the cream of the German squad is going to prove to be a little more taxing …

Saturday June 17th

The nerves are too much. The whole country's on tenterhooks, and it's all down to my dad – and a few of the other boys in the team, admittedly. I was thinking of offering my services for tonight's match, as I seem to be dribbling more effectively than ever; but I'm not one to try and steal my Dad's thunder. But you'd better win, Dad. If you don't win, I might be forced to scream incessantly, night after night, as loud as my little lungs will allow, for several weeks.

No pressure, of course.

Sunday June 18th

ONE-NIL! ONE-NIL ONE-NIL ONE-

NIL! (To us, incidentally.)

As you can tell, dear diary, I am entering into the almost unbearably exciting national fever that has gripped the country in the wake of our noble defeat of the Germans. Not that I want to appear competitive in any way, but, um, how can I put this – Eat my shorts, dudes!

Monday June 19th

That was my dad out there on the pitch! You shoulda seen me when the final whistle blew – I ran round the sofa (well, I ran halfway round the sofa, fell on my bum, cried, got Mum to put me on my feet again, giggled, completed my circuit, fell on my bum again – you get the idea …) and squealed with such delight anyone would have thought Baby Spice had asked me to marry her. It's times like this that make you proud to be a Beckham.

Tuesday June 20th

Game number three tonight, against Romania. Given our world-class performance the other night, we can't lose...

Wednesday June 21st

... or maybe we can. England 2, Romania 3. I'm afraid the wind has been taken out of my sails somewhat. Poor old Dad's in a right old state because it means he won't win the European Championship. Not even one of my cheeky little smiles can cheer him up ...

Thursday June 22nd

Aw, c'mon Dad, cheer up. Don't get your knickers in a twist. In fact, just leave the knickers alone full stop, would you?

Friday June 23rd

Dad's still moping, I'm afraid. I wish he'd brighten up – it's only a game after all. It's not like the Big Bad Evil Ginger One has cast an horrific curse on you or anything.

Saturday June 24th

Talking of the Evil Ginger One, Dad had better get started on his book. I've been giving it some serious thought, and I think that this is my one chance to scupper Ginger Spice's plans. Clearly her book is a way of spreading her evil philosophy. I'm going to have to use my influence over Dad to ensure that his book counteracts the evil gospel that the Ginger One has already spread across the world.

So you see, the whole project – *David Beckham: My World* – has become more important than anybody could have possibly imagined. Dad, the safety of the world's in your hands!

Sunday June 25th

Depressing thought, isn't it …

Monday June 26th

Phew! It looks like Dad's muscling down to it. Actually, it's thanks to Mum – she's forcing him to sit down at the kitchen table with some blank paper and his new pen, and start writing.

I've never seen such a look of desperate concentration on a man's face before.

Tuesday June 27th

He's still sitting there. I don't think he's written anything yet, but he *is* still sitting there.

Wednesday June 28th

Cripes, the tension is really getting to me. Dad almost put pen to paper at about lunchtime, but he started hyperventilating before he could manage it. Mum gave him a cup of warm milk and a Jammie Dodger and he calmed down a bit, fortunately. He's back at the kitchen table now, scratching his head.

Thursday June 29th

C'mon Dad, you can do it!

Friday June 30th

He nearly did it! He was so close. Me and Mum were sitting around watching him, giving him the sort of moral support that it's only proper he should expect from a close-knit, loving family unit. And then it happened: his pen moved towards the paper; Mum let out a little gasp; the whole world seemed to hold its breath; and then Dad looked up and uttered the words I shall never forget as long as I live – 'Victoria, how do you spell "Chapter One"?'

This whole business could take a great deal longer than I'd previously anticipated …

JULY
2000

Saturday July 1st

An inauspicious start to the month. Dad seems to have gone off the rails a bit in the old book-writing department. He got as far as writing 'My name is', but he fell at the first post when he couldn't spell 'David'. A fat lot of good this is going to be as an antidote to the work of the Big Bad Evil Ginger One; more to the point, there's a load of dough riding on him producing something, and Gucci nappies don't come cheap these days. He'd better get his nose to the grindstone.

Sunday July 2nd

Tomorrow is Mum and Dad's wedding anniversary. Tomorrow they celebrate an entire year of wedded bliss. Personally, I hope they're not going to do too much celebrating – I don't want to appear to be a killjoy, but it really doesn't seem to me to be entirely appropriate. After all, what they'd essentially be celebrating is that disastrous day a year ago when I was presented to the world in a cissy-looking purple dress. I overheard them talking about the possibility of shoving me in it again, as some kind of hugely misplaced nostalgia trip, but fortunately I've completely outgrown the horrible thing now.

Nope, it's their paper wedding anniversary, and I hope they celebrate by blowing a bit of paper money on some much-needed outfits for yours truly. I haven't had any new clothes for at least a week, after all …

Monday July 3rd

Hurrumph! We're going out to a Chinese restaurant tonight to celebrate. I'm sorry if I sound a bit peeved, but frankly I don't see the point of my going to these fancy joints – I never get a chance to sample the indigenous tuck, if you know what I mean.

No sign of any extravagant present yet – I'll have to fill you in tomorrow. Still, pleased to report that I haven't been forced to wear a shred of purple all day.

Tuesday July 4th

Zowee! Dad's got his weak points, I know, but you've got to hand it to him. When it comes to splashing the cash, he doesn't hold back.

The start of the evening was a bit ropey.

Mum and Dad ordered a load of food, but they weren't too thrilled when it turned up. Mum called the waiter over in her usual bossy manner, and said, 'Oi, this is bloody rubbery!' The waiter flashed her a charming smile and said, 'Thank you velly much,' before moving off to serve someone else. Between you and me, I think they were a bit nonplussed, so they shut up and ate what they were given. Best of all though, I got to try a bit! Mum asked, 'Would you like an ickle bit of Crispy Fried Duck?' Dad said 'Yes please' before Mum gave him one of her looks and fed me with my first-ever mouthful of proper solids.

What a relief! It's taken them long enough to get round to letting me eat like a normal human being. I felt like grabbing the opportunity of their generosity by ordering a plateful of truffled sweetbreads, but unfortunately my linguistic limitations let me down. However, I did manage to reward them with another word, and a significant one at that – 'Brooklyn!'

Yep! Word number two, my lords, ladies and gentlemen, is 'Brooklyn'. It's only a short step from here to 'Big it up', and before you know it I'll be jabbering away with the best of them.

So once Mum and Dad had gone all goggle-eyed over my new-found vocabulary, Dad pulled out the prezzie. Talk about coming up with the goods: a brand spanking new diamond ring - £50,000 worth of top-notch rock.

Wednesday July 5th

Fifty grand! I'm still reeling from the flashness of it all. To put it into some kind of context, that's about five thousand servings of Crispy Duck – ah, the luxury of being able to draw a more adult comparison …

Thursday July 6th

I've got to admit it – there's a great deal I can learn from my daddio. Mum's been on cloud nine ever since he gave her that ring. She's so chuffed, she's told him that he can record backing vocals on her new song.

Dad's pleased as punch, although personally I think she might be making a bit of a mistake – Dad really isn't known for his musical ability.

Friday July 7th

Come to think of it, that never stopped Mum. But it doesn't mean Dad's the ideal choice by any stretch of the imagination – I heard him practising his singing in the shower this morning; Lordy me, you never heard such a racket.

I'm a bit hurt Mum didn't offer me the gig, to be honest, angelic little cherub that I am.

Saturday July 8th

Mum's new song is called 'Out Of Your Mind'.

Did I say anything? Well, did I?

Sunday July 9th

Oh dearie dear. Mum's got a big concert in Hyde Park tonight. Dad's getting a bit carried away with the old pop star thing and wants to go on stage with her. Respect to my ma, she's put her foot down and told him he can jolly well wait backstage with me. Apparently, we get to meet Prince Charles – I imagine he's quite looking forward to rubbing shoulders with royalty …

Monday July 10th

Now that's what I call a gig! Mum was top of the bill, of course, and unfortunately she got a bit of flak for miming to her record.

Quite why, I've yet to work out – I can absolutely guarantee that it sounded a lot better than when she's actually singing. Why on earth would they want her to do that, I wonder? Still, she got a groovy kind of response – almost as much cheering as when I took to the pitch at Old Trafford. Almost, you note – not quite.

So then it was backstage to meet Bonnie Prince Charlie. Blimey – if you think my mum's Posh, you should cop a load of this geezer. We all stood in a line, and he came and shook Mum and Dad's hands and had a few words:

Prince Chaz: *Delighted to meet you again, Mrs Spice.*
Mum: *Delighted to meet you again too, your Royal Sovereign Highness.*
Prince Chaz: *And one is equally delighted to meet your little boy. Tell me,*

*has he started learning how to kick a
ball yet?*

Mum*: Yeah, a little bit, your Worshipful
Majesty.*

Prince Chaz*: Excellent. And what about
Brooklyn?*

The conversation went a bit downhill
from there. Prince Chaz asked Dad how his
book was coming along, and looked a bit
shocked when Dad told him he thought it
would pick up once he'd mastered the
alphabet. I do wish he'd keep his mouth
shut sometimes. It really doesn't reflect well
on me ...

Tuesday July 11th

I gotta say, with my newly learned vocal
skills, I'm wondering if it might be a good
career move to be a pop star. I'd always
assumed that footy superstardom was the
way for me, but I must admit that seeing

Mum the other night gave me a taste for the unthinking adulation that only a pop star can create. I must give it some serious thought.

Wednesday July 12th

Dad's got his shoulder back to the wheel with the old book-writing. We've got someone coming round to take the photos tomorrow – better make sure I'm looking my sexy best. And he'd better take lots of photos – I've got a feeling Dad's going to need all the padding he can get.

Thursday July 13th

Ah, there's nothing like an extensive photo shoot to boost a kiddie's ego. I've been snapped every which way you care to imagine – and for once, Mum didn't dress me up like a girl. Or a clown. Dad looked a bit odd, but hey, it's his book, his decision.

Best of all, the photographer took absolutely squillions of pics, so the pressure's off Dad a bit. He seems much happier, bless him.

Friday July 14th

Oo-er … The video for Mum's new song has been causing quite a fuss. In it, she dresses up in all these spooky clothes and pretends to be like something from a horror movie. Frankly, I can't seen why everyone's so concerned – she doesn't look all that bad to me. But then, I suppose I have seen her first thing in the morning before she slaps on the old lippie. Scary ain't the word – it's enough to make you tremble in your booties …

Saturday July 15th

Hurrah! We're off on holiday on Thursday. I must say, I could use a break; after all, I haven't been away for a good six weeks or so. And Dad could definitely use a change of scene – he's been looking a bit drawn, thanks to the constant toil he's been putting in on his book.

Sunday July 16th

I hope all his hard work pays off; and I hope he has written a lengthy and eloquent sermon denouncing the works of the evil Ginger Spice.

Monday July 17th

Hmmm … The more I think about it, the more unlikely it seems. Perhaps I'd better give him a helping hand.

Tuesday July 18th

BROOKLYN'S DENUNCIATION OF
THE BIG BAD EVIL GINGER ONE
Know ye, my people, that the spawn of evil is amongst us. A thing more gruesome and

more terrifying than any that man has yet encountered. And no, I'm not talking about Mum's new single. Or Dad's haircut. Beware the Evil Ginger One, she that has erred from the path of Spiciness and been doomed to wail tunelessly in the void for the rest of her days. Her work comes in many and varied guises, but remember: that which seems sweet and sugary on the outside can often prove rotten to the core ...

It's pretty serious stuff, I know, but people have got to be made aware of the danger they're in. All I've got to do now is think of a way to get Dad to work my warning into his book ...

Wednesday July 19th

Off on our holly-dollies tomorrow – St Tropez here we come. The diary, as usual, will have to stay safe at home, away from prying eyes. I dread to think what would happen if it got into the wrong hands …

Thursday July 20th

Friday July 21st

Saturday July 22nd

Sunday July 23rd

Monday July 24th

Tuesday July 25th

Wednesday July 26th

Thursday July 27th

Home again, tanned, healthy, and, dare I say it, even a little sexier than when I left. I must say, I have a soft spot for the South of France – it matches my Mediterranean temperament rather well, I think.

We stayed at the villa of a funny little man

called Mr Al Fayed. Between you and me, dear diary, he's not much to look at, but I have a horrible suspicion that he might be richer even than Mum and Dad. He invited us on to his yacht, and even Mum seemed impressed with the lavishness of it all.

After a few days there, it was off to stay with Mum and Dad's friend John Elton (they will insist on calling him by his surname, which, to be honest, I find a little gauche). He's a nice enough lad, I suppose, but I wish he wouldn't spend so much time pinching Dad's bottom. Ho hum, I guess you have to take the rough with the smooth – not that Dad's bottom is particularly smooth (at least, not compared to mine ...)

Friday July 28th

The break's clearly done Dad the world of good. He's writing at a rate of knots – comparatively speaking. He spent all morning with his pen and paper, and I sneaked a look at his work:

Chapter Too

I like footbal very much. I think its grate. And I like Viktorya very much. I think she is grate aswel.

It's riveting stuff, you've gotta admit ...

Saturday July 29th

Hmmm ... Come to think of it, I notice there was no mention of me in that little family treatise. I hope Dad thinks I'm grate too. Maybe he's saving that for Chapter Free.

Sunday July 30th

The more I think about it, the gladder I am that that photographer took plenty of snaps. On the basis of the evidence before us, we're gonna need all the help we can get!

Monday July 31st

And so we draw to the end of another month. All in all it's been pretty eventful – I've continued my battle against the Evil Ginger One, I've been introduced to royalty, I've eaten my first solid food. My life gets more and more hectic by the minute. Let's hope August calms down a bit …

AUGUST
2000

Tuesday August 1st

Way to go! I'm really getting the hang of this speaking malarkey. As of lunchtime today, not only can I manage 'No' and 'Brooklyn', my repertoire has extended to 'Yes', 'Ma', 'Da' and 'Plop'.

Clearly I'll have to avoid 'Plop' in any but the most casual social situations, but for now I think I'm going to have to practise what I've got as a sound base from which to grow. With my extensive range of coos, giggles and idiomatic dribbling, I'm turning into quite an expressive dude ...

Wednesday August 2nd

'Yes, Ma! Plop!'

Thursday August 3rd

'Coo ... giggle ... Da Da Plop Plop!'

Friday August 4th

'Brooklyn plop yes? 'OH FOR HEAVEN'S SAKE, DAD, WILL YOU STOP TALKING TO ME LIKE THAT? DO I LOOK LIKE AN IDIOT????

Saturday August 5th

That's better. Dad's got back to work on his book, which leaves me alone to practise my speaking. It's about time I hooked up with Phoenix Chi again – she'll be knocked out with the progress I've made.

Sunday August 6th

Knocked out or sick as a dog with jealousy. Ha ha ha!!

Monday August 7th

Mum's sulking. I can't make my mind up whether or not I like it. On the plus side, she keeps her trap shut, which is always a bonus. But on the minus side, it means Dad has to do the cooking. That's enough to make anyone lose the will to live, so Mum gets even sulkier – it's a vicious circle, spiralling out of control ...

Anyway, the reason for today's little barney? Dad's banned Mum from wearing mini-skirts. He says it's because he doesn't want me to be embarrassed by people coming up and saying, 'I've seen your mum's knickers.'

Well, Dad, I appreciate the thought, I

really do, but I'm afraid it's a case of too little too late. I gave up all hopes of not being embarrassed by my folks years ago – well, one year ago, if you're splitting hairs.

Tuesday August 8th

Come to think of it, I didn't know Mum had any mini-skirts. She's got quite a lot of what look to me like fancy spangly belts, but surely he can't mean those?

Wednesday August 9th

Maybe he does. If Mum takes those belts off, you *can* see her knickers, and I can't help thinking that Dad does have an unhealthy fascination with Mum's smalls.

Honestly, grown-ups! I'll never understand them. I mean, if Dad likes knickers so much, why does he make such a fuss about changing my nappies? C'mon dude, a bit of consistency, if you please ...

Thursday August 10th

Oh dear. Mum really is sulking. She's just given an interview to a newspaper to say that Dad's an animal in bed. How demeaning can you get? She's got a point, though – you should hear him snoring. He does bear a passing resemblance to a water buffalo with sinusitis. But it's really not nice to tell everyone about it, Mum.

Friday August 11th

You know, I really will never understand these two. Dad seems absolutely delighted by Mum's latest *faux-pas*. He seems to actively like been referred to as an animal – he's all over Mum. Ah well, whatever melts your butter, my friend. Personally I live in hope that Mum will refer to me in the press in a slightly more dignified manner …

Saturday August 12th

Phewee, what a lucky little chappie I am. Mum's going to somewhere called Ibiza to play some concerts, and guess who gets to go along – *moi*. Dad's staying at home to polish off his book, although how he's going to manage without someone around to remind him which hand to put his pen in is anybody's guess.

Anyway, the long and the short of it is that I'm off on yet another of my worldwide tours – I'll fill you in as soon as I'm back, dear diary.

Sunday August 13th
Monday August 14th
Tuesday August 15th
Wednesday August 16th

Thursday August 17th
Friday August 18th
Saturday August 19th

Wickeeeeed!!!! A massive alo goin' out to you, dear diary. I've been 'avin' it large in Ibiza, and loved every minute. This dude was born to party – ah, the sun, the sea, the chicks (sorry Baby Spice – but you know what they say: it don't matter where you get your appetite, as long as you dine at home ...)

Of course, there was the odd glitch, as usual – we arrived in Ibiza in good time, but Mum's luggage went to Barcelona; she got a bit stressed out over that, but all's well that ends well – she cheered up after we managed to charter a big enough plane to get it all back to her. We checked into our nice big hotel – an intimate little group of us (just five bodyguards, two stylists and a personal chef – and that was just for me – you should have seen the number of people Mum brought along).

Mum was star of the show, of course. The whole island was buzzing to hear her do her gig. She sang (well, I use the term in its broadest possible sense) her new song 'Out Of Your Mind' and the audience duly went out of theirs.

Sunday August 20th

The more I think about it, the more I wanna be a rock 'n' roll star. Footy's all very well, but if you don't score a goal, it seems to me that the gig's a write-off. With Mum, she gets the payback in terms of audience adulation every time she walks on stage. I'll have a bit of that, please.

Monday August 21st

Dad was absolutely delighted to see us

home, but he was even more excited to give us the good news he's obviously been bottling up. As soon as we walked through the door, he couldn't help himself blurting out, 'I know it's taken me ages, but I've finished my book!' I was about to tell him that I was a slow reader myself, but then the full magnitude of what he'd said dawned on me!

Yep! He's actually finished his *magnum opus*! Dad, I'm proud of you. People said it couldn't be done – even I had my moments of doubt, I've got to admit – but you rose above the criticism and produced a significant and enduring work of art. Years from now, I'll be able to show it to my grandchildren (d'ya hear that, Baby?) and tell them that I was around at the inception of this land mark of world literature.

OK, so it's a bit short, but hey, short can be good. I'm a bit on the small side myself, but you can't deny that I'm perfectly formed. Oh, and there's quite a lot of crossing out, but I'm sure that won't be a problem. OK, OK, so the spelling's a bit ropey, but you can't have everything. I'm sure it's gonna be a corker – and I've no doubt it's going to knock the Big Bad Evil Ginger One's evil testament into the ether. Ah well, we live in hope ...

Tuesday August 22nd

Mum's new single is out in the shops. She seems to be very keen for it to go to number 1. Dad asked her how she was going to make sure it did the biz, and she said, 'Publicity, obviously. Plus I've got a couple of little tricks up my sleeve ...'

This makes me very, very nervous, dear diary. I hate it when she goes into one of her publicity drives, for the simple reason that she opens her big gob and says the most embarrassing things.

Oh well, better sit tight ...

And I wonder what tricks she's got up her sleeve. I overheard her talking to Scary Spice on the phone, and I gotta say I'm completely confused. 'I know Madonna does it in a big truck,' she said, 'and Britney Spears likes to use a transit van. Robbie Williams does it in a little Mini, and it hasn't seemed to have done him much harm.' What the heck is she talking about?????

Wednesday August 23rd

Mum went out first thing this morning and came back well after tea-time, driving a great big van. She wandered into the house and said, all innocently, 'David, I bought a few records today. You, er, couldn't pop them in the garage for me, could you?' Dad started to explain that he was in the middle of a game of peek-a-boo with me, but Mum just said, 'Now, David!' and off he went.

What's the point of buying records and putting them in the garage? It's a mystery to me ...

Thursday August 24th

Hmmm ... Same deal today. What *is* Mum up to?

Friday August 25th

OK, Mum, spill the beans. Every day she goes out, buys a truckload of records, and gets Dad to put them in the garage. He had to move the Porsche out to fit them in.

And the Ferrari ...

And the Mercedes ...

There was just enough room for the Range Rover to stay, but if Mum carries on like this, that's gonna have to go too.

Maybe she's preparing to educate Dad in the ways of good music. It must be said, his record collection could do with a bit of expansion:

Dad's Record Collection
Garage Mastercuts Volume 4
Spice Girls, collected works
Manchester United Team Songs
1970-2000
Sing Along with Noddy

He used to have a few All Saints CDs, but Mum gently suggested that he might like to ritually burn them in a pentangle, and he wisely agreed.

So yes, the lad needs a bit of a musical education, but I think Mum might be going over the top a bit …

Saturday August 26th

Mum's very on edge. We were listening to the radio today, and the DJ said that a song by somebody called Spiller was looking likely to become number 1. Mum went a bit tight lipped, told Dad to look after me, and off she went. She hasn't come back yet, but I have a sneaking suspicion I know what she'll have with her when she does …

Sunday August 27th

Yep! A van full of records. A terrible suspicion is dawning on me. Could my ma possibly be trying to, ahem, rationalise the statistics of the pop world by buying up copies of her own record? Life is full of surprises, wouldn't you say? I had no idea this is how the business works.

Does Mrs Madonna really do it in a big truck? Well, I really thing Mum ought to get something a bit swankier to do it in – a helicopter, maybe, or a jumbo jet. OK, so it'd be a bit tricky to park in the high street, but she has an image to maintain after all. Good job I'm here to advise her. When I'm a major international pop mega-star, will I have to do this too? If so, I'll certainly make sure I get a bigger van than the one Mum's using – why do these things by halves, after all?

I must try and sneak a look in the garage to confirm my theory.

Monday August 28th

Well, I've seen it with my own eyes – there must be, at a conservative estimate, several grillion copies of Mum's record in the garage. Mum's acting a bit sheepish about the whole thing. Every time Dad asks when he can put his cars back, she says, 'Just shut up, David,' and goes and takes her frustrations out on the piano.

Dad's learned rather quickly to stop mentioning it. He catches on pretty quick …

Tuesday August 29th

We find out tomorrow if Mum's hit the top

spot. The tension is unbearable …

Wednesday August 30th

Disaster! Such wailing and a-gnashing of teeth has seldom been seen within the hallowed walls of Beckingham Palace (with the possible exception of the time Dad was so busy Brylcreaming his hair that he forgot to change my nappy – boy, I let them know about that …)

As you may have guessed, dear diary, Mum failed to hit numero uno. She said some very unpleasant things about Spiller, the band who beat her, that I blush to record in this diary. Suffice to say, what she suggested sounds very uncomfortable.

Dad's doing his best to cheer her up, bless him, but he's not getting very far. If you'll excuse me, I think perhaps I could be of use trying to take her mind off things – perhaps I'll go and break something, or maybe create a diversion with one of my noisier toys.

Y'know, sometimes I feel like they're the kids around here.

Thursday August 31st

On second thoughts, maybe that wasn't such a good idea – I've had my baby drum kit confiscated. I'm not too worried, though – Dad can't resist playing on it, so I'm sure it'll put in an appearance reasonably soon. But Mum's certainly in a bit of a tizz about the whole affair. Dad's not really helping. I overheard him say (in an icky kind of voice), 'Don't worry, darling. You'll always be my number 1!' Mum gave him a very condescending look, and I spent the next half-hour looking for the sick bag.

I really, really hope her next record does a bit better. Maybe if Dad buys her an articulated lorry, she'll be in with more of a chance...

SEPTEMBER 2000

Friday September 1st

Mum's still terribly cross. She didn't get out of bed today, because she said she had a headache. I heard Dad mutter, 'When don't you,' but I did notice that he went out of his way to make sure Mum didn't hear him. I really don't know what he's on about, to be honest – she hardly ever complains of a headache when I'm around.

Saturday September 2nd

I'm really getting rather worried. Mum

doesn't look well at all, and she didn't even respond properly to one of my most charming giggles – a sure sign that something's wrong …

Sunday September 3rd

Help! Mum's got to go to hospital. The doctor says she's got something called viral meningitis – no idea what it is, but it sounds absolutely terrifying. They took her off in an ambulance this morning, leaving me in Dad's tender care. The poor lad's in an even worse state than I am, but we Beckham males have got to be strong in our darkest hour …

Monday September 4th

Sweet Mother, there are so many things I neglected to tell you before you were so untimely wrested from me by the fickle hand of fate. Don't get me wrong, Dad's great, but no matter how often he dresses up in your underwear, he really can't take your place. When he draws me to his breast to comfort me, frankly he lacks the soothing plumpness that I have grown to love. When he gives me my bath, it's always gone cold by the time he's worked out how to open the bottle of baby shampoo.

Come back, Mum – your little boy needs you!

Tuesday September 5th

And you should taste Dad's cooking – Mum, come back to me and I'll never mention the mashed food hell of my early year ever again. Promise!

Wednesday September 6th

Oh no, this is really getting serious. Apparently Mum's going to pull through, but the doctors are worried that *I* might have caught something 'orrible. Last time I was in hospital, I got pampered by all the cutie nurses. This time I might not be so lucky …

The doc's coming round tomorrow to check me out …

Thursday September 7th

Aw, gerroff!!! I've been prodded and poked all over the shop – honestly, these doctors have no sense of how to respect a dude's privacy. Anyway, the good news is I've got the all clear – and the even better news is that Mum gets to come back in a couple of days. What a welcome she's going to get!

Friday September 8th

Ah, Dad's so excited. He's been going round the house spring-cleaning with his feather duster – on this occasion, I've even let him get away with wearing a girly apron

(although I did make a mental note of how keen he was to put it on ...)

Saturday September 9th

Welcome home, Mum! Boy am I glad to see her back. It was rather a touching scene when she walked back through the door and got caught up in Dad's arms – I know he can be a goon, but he's an affectionate old thing really.

She's gone off to bed to relax a bit. I think I'll spend a few hours colouring in my wallpaper.

Sunday September 10th

Oh dear. I think the sooner Mum's fit enough to go back to work the better. They've been slouching around chatting about other ways that they can earn an extra crust. Of course in their case it wouldn't be so much a crust as the entire loaf. Hell, they'd probably buy up the bakery. Ordinarily, of course, I'd be all for this – but they really shouldn't be allowed to come up with these schemes for themselves. The latest Beckham masterplan, it seems, is some kind of merchandising deal. Quite what they're going to merchandise is anyone's guess …

Monday September 11th

I might have bleedin' known it! Dad wants to license a David Beckham bandanna! Why not go the whole hog? Ladies and gentleman, the David Beckham sarong – it looks like a skirt, you wear it like a skirt, but no, it says David Beckham on it so it's a sarong. Or the Becks Thong, perhaps? Looks remarkably similar to the Posh Thong, but who's worrying about that?

Not those two, obviously.

Tuesday September 12th

A terrible thought has just crossed my mind. I can't even bring myself to write about it.

Wednesday September 13th

Mum! Dad! Don't do it to me, I beg of you!

Thursday September 14th

What if they're thinking of Baby Brooklyn merchandise? How will I live it down? Just imagine – the Baby Brooklyn potty; Baby Brooklyn nappies. It would all be too much …

Friday September 15th

I guess I could live with a 'Brooklyn Beckham' designer label, but the chances of me being able to decide on the range are pretty close to zero – trust me. Knowing Mum, she'd choose a girly combination of pinks and purples, and before I know where I am I'll be the laughing stock of the fashion world. Mum reckons she's a catwalk cutie, but entre nous, my dear diary, she hasn't got a clue.

Saturday September 16th

And what would Baby Spice think of it all? She's coming round to pay a visit to my dear recuperating mother tomorrow – I'd better warn her in advance, and make sure she understands that if the worst happens it'll be outta my hands …

Sunday September 17th

Well, she seemed pretty sympathetic, but to be honest you can never tell with these chicks.

Baby Spice: *How's my favourite little boy today, then?*

Brooklyn: *That's right, gorgeous, give in to your desires. You know they're too strong to resist. But, since you ask, I got a coupla things on my mind. They say communication is the basis of all enduring relationships, so I thought perhaps you wouldn't mind me sounding you out on a few minor matters ...*

Baby Spice: *Oooh, I could eat you up!*

Brooklyn: *Later, already! Listen, if you and me are gonna make a try of this, you've gotta realise that there's a time for passion, and a time for talkin'. I know you're only human, but try and keep your libido in check, huh? Now, I got this sneaking suspicion that the Oldies are going to start manufacturing Brooklyn dolls or some such nonsense. You could see what an awkward position that would put me in, now ...*

Baby Spice: *Yes I could, yes I could, yes I could!*

Brooklyn: *Good. I just want to be sure that ritual humiliation by the Oldies, no matter how well meaning they might be, won't be an impediment to our love ...*

Baby Spice: *What an adorable thing you are!*

Well, I took that to mean she'd be able to handle it if it happened. She's got a good head on her shoulders, that Baby Spice. Beautiful and with a brain to match. What a catch! Sometimes I forget how lucky I am...

Monday September 18th

All quiet on the merchandising front, I'm pleased to report. I hope it was just a moment of misplaced enthusiasm.

Mum seems to have made a complete

recovery, and a good thing too. The potential for disaster when she and Dad are left to their own devices is just too great. She's giving a newspaper an interview tomorrow, fortunately, so at least we're back on the path to normality.

Tuesday September 19th

Aaaarrrggghh! You would not believe what Mum just said to that journalist. I can't even bring myself to record it in my diary. All I can do is live in constant hope that her comments will never see the light of day …

I know, I know – it's unlikely. But I can dream, can't I?

Wednesday September 20th

That's it! That is it! I am now, officially, the most embarrassed toddler in the entire Western world. And if there's a toddler more embarrassed than me in the Eastern world, I'd like to see them.

Seeing as it's been plastered all over the newspapers today, I see no harm in recording exactly what it was Mum said to that pesky hack. Even if you tried to guess, dear diary, you'd never come up with something so excruciating. Not only did she say that my dad likes being a gay icon, she said that he actually enjoys flirting with men.

Need I elaborate on my humiliation?

Thursday September 21st

Aw no! Dad's really not taking this awful turn of events seriously. He's spent the day wearing next to nothing, and skipping round the kitchen singing, 'I'm a gay icon! I'm a gay icon!' Mum thinks it's hilarious. I haven't bawled so much for months.

Friday September 22nd

You'd think some of my inherent dignity would have rubbed off on him, wouldn't you. Well, nope, it seems not.

Saturday September 23rd

If he calls my luvvie one more time, I think I'll scream.

Sunday September 24th

There's just one cure for it. I'm going to have to ban Mum and Dad from giving any more interviews in the future. If anybody wants to know anything about life behind the walls of Beckingham Palace, they'll have to come to me.

Monday September 25th

Admittedly my limited vocabulary (currently approximately twenty words) might get in the way, but let's face it – a short interview is better than a stupid one.

Tuesday September 26th

It's only just dawned on me – maybe that reporter was a disciple of She Who Must Not Be Named, sent to bring down the greatness of the House of Beckham by prying and revealing our most intimate secrets and exposing our innate vulnerability.

Wednesday September 27th

Or maybe Mum's just a bit of a plonker. Yeah, sounds more likely to me ...

Thursday September 28th

There's been a great big newspaper report saying that Mum's had nine haircuts in nine months, and that they cost £50,000.

I'm giving serious thought to ditching the

pop star idea and becoming a hairdresser. My last haircut took precisely two minutes (it doesn't take long to take it all off). If my calculations are correct, that means the going rate for a hairdresser is getting on for two-and-a-half grand a minute. That's more than even my Mum and Dad earn, put together!!!

Friday September 29th

Yep, the more I think about it, the more I like it. It would even clinch the deal with Baby Spice, I reckon – she wouldn't be able to resist a dude who was a) as sexy as me, and b) could sort her hair out should it ever become dishevelled. Not that I can possibly imagine how that could happen, you understand …

Saturday September 30th

I'll check out the hairdressing idea with

Phoenix Chi when she comes round tomorrow. In fact, I've got quite a lot of stuff I need to discuss with her – I hope she's feeling chatty!

OCTOBER 2000

Sunday October 1st

My whole world has crumbled! Everything I had previously held to be true has been turned on its head! My life will never be the same again …

Forgive me, dear diary, if I am unable to elaborate. I'll fill you in when I'm able to come to terms with today's disastrous intelligence.

Monday October 2nd

I don't know what to believe any more.

Friend and foe have merged into one.

Tuesday October 3rd

Phoenix Chi! Can it be that all this time you've been a wolf in sheep's clothing?

Wednesday October 4th

(Not that there's anything wrong with sheep's clothing – I've got a swish little sheepskin jacket myself which, I'm not afraid to say, makes me look rather dashing ...)

Thursday October 5th

As you may have deduced, Sunday's meeting with Phoenix Chi was eventful, to say the least. Scary Spice brought her round, and as she and Mum were having a natter over coffee and biscuits (Mum ate a whole custard cream, which I thought was overdoing it a bit ...) I decided to sound PC out over the hairdresser idea:

Brooklyn: *Hey, PC!*

Phoenix Chi: *Phoenix Chi's the name, dude. You don't want me to start callin' you Brookers, now do you?*

Brooklyn: *Hmmm … good point. OK, Phoenix Chi, I gotta tell you my latest career plan.*

Phoenix Chi: *What's it to be? Rocket scientist? Astrophysicist? Dude, I hate to break it to you like this, but look at your old man …*

Brooklyn: *OK, OK, there's no need to get personal. Actually, I was thinking more along the lines of being a hairdresser. You should see the amount Mum pays hers …*

I took PC's prolonged attack of helpless mirth to be an indication that she did not see eye to eye with me on the matter; ordinarily I would have taken on board her comments (not that there were many comments – just giggles), but then she dropped the bombshell on me that was to change our relationship for ever. We were gently discussing our respective love lives, when she came out with the words I'd never have expected to hear from her wise old lips:

Phoenix Chi: *Y'know kid, if I were in your shoes – nice shoes, by the way …*

Brooklyn: *Thanks. Gucci …*

Phoenix Chi: *… classy, dude, classy. Anyway, like I was sayin', if I were in your shoes, I'd say that Ginger Spice was worth a second look.*

Brooklyn: *[Profound look of dumbfounded shock, horror and bewilderment.]*

Phoenix Chi: *Yeah, I know, I know, it's a bit of an about turn, but I seen pictures of her lately. She's looking kinda foxy ...*
Brooklyn: *[Utter silence ...]*
Phoenix Chi: *... and the kids love her. Yeah, I reckon maybe we were a bit hasty in listening to our mums about how completely evil she is ...*

Need I say more?

Friday October 6th

Clearly Phoenix Chi has come under the Big Bad Evil Ginger One's pernicious spell. How am I to fight her terrifying influence when even my closest ally has fallen to her?

Saturday October 7th

That it should come to this. That I should have to look to my own sweet father to aid me in my fight against the forces of the

Dark One. His book gets released in a few days; I can only pray that it will prove to be a powerful weapon in the eternal struggle of good against evil.

Sunday October 8th

Well! I gotta say it, sometimes my dear old dad surprises me. I never thought he'd be up to it, but clearly there's more to him than meets the eye (actually, there'd kinda have to be, I suppose). Copies of his book arrived today, and I can't deny it's quite a dishy-looking product. It seems all the blood, sweat and tears (and writer's block and head-scratching and learning the alphabet) that went into its creation has finally paid off.

My dad! A famous author. And though I say so myself, the piccies inside rather do me justice.

The only downside, in my humble

opinion, is the cover – a bit of a dodgy close-up of the old boy, all drenched in red. If I ever write a book, you wouldn't catch me bunging an image like that on the front. Man U kit aside, red really isn't my colour...

Monday October 9th

Blimey! Who'd have thought the day would arrive that Dad would have serious respect from the literary establishment. It said in the papers today that Dad's book was 'a significant work from the leading light behind Manchester United's continuing success'! Howzabout that, ladies and gentlemen?

Mum's dead chuffed. She keeps pinching Dad's bottom and calling him 'my little Shakespeare'.

Let's not overstate the case, eh Mum?

Tuesday October 10th

OK, Dad, the book's great and everything, but let's not let it go to your head. He's been walking around with a furrowed brow, rubbing his chin learnedly and with a pen tucked behind his ear.

I hate to burst his bubble, but he's got to stop thinking of himself in this light …

Wednesday October 11th

Ah, that's better. Mum noticed the seedlings of Dad's literary pretensions and nipped them quickly in the bud by asking him to write the shopping list.

He's gone back to playing footy in the garden …

Thursday October 12th

Caught Mum and Dad talking about the book last night. They seem terribly keen for it to do well. Mum told Dad that he'd have to jolly well get out there and sign lots of copies; but Dad just gave her an enigmatic smile and told her he had a better idea ...

Friday October 13th

I'm feeling very nervous. Let us not forget that Dad's last good idea was to engineer our respective coiffeurs so that we looked like a couple of Mekons.

He's been out all day. And on Friday the 13th, as well. Anything could happen. I wish I knew what he was up to ...

Saturday October 14th

Hmmm ... he came back last night with a van full of boxes, which he stacked up next to Mum's records in the garage.

Sunday October 15th

Same thing last night. This is beginning to

have a ring of familiarity about it …

Monday October 16th

Dad had difficulty shutting the garage door this morning. He asked Mum if they could throw out some of her records, but she gave him one of her looks and he backed down.

I can't help thinking that Dad's taken a leaf out of the Posh Spice manual of commercial success. I'll have to have a toddle out to the garage at some stage to determine if my suspicions are correct …

Tuesday October 17th

Aaawwwww Dad!!!!!!!!!!!! Sometimes I just despair. Sometimes I wonder if we can possibly be related – me: streetwise, savvy, a good head on my little shoulders. And Dad: sweet enough, it's true; but with about as much common sense as a tube of Smarties.

Mum and Dad were busy canoodling in

the front room earlier on, so I had a sneaky peek in the garage. I can't tell you what a relief it is to have a bit of mobility – you find out all sorts of interesting stuff. And what did I find out today? Only that Dad's been buying the wrong bleedin' book. Yes, dear diary, the Beckham household is now the proud owner of about fifteen zillion copies of, well, I don't know what exactly. I'm too little to be able to see inside the boxes very well, but one thing I do know – Dad's book's red; whatever's in the garage ain't.

Wednesday October 18th

Mum's going to be furious. I hope she doesn't find out – I need my peace and quiet …

Thursday October 19th

Oh dear, oh dear, oh dear. Dad got a bit of a grilling over breakfast:

Mum: *David, you know those boxes in the garage?*

Dad: *[Sheepishly] Yeah?*

Mum: *What's in them, David?*

Dad: *Well, actually they're all part of my cunning plan.*

Mum: *And what cunning plan is that, then?*

Dad: *Well, over the last few days I've been going out in disguise …*

Mum: *In disguise?*

Dad: *Yeah, I've been wearing trousers for a change. Anyway, I've gone in to lots of shops and asked for all the copies they've got of the book by 'the leading light behind Manchester United's continuing success'.*

Mum: *I see, David. Is that why our garage is full of books by that ghastly little Alex Ferguson?*

Trust Dad! Mum tried to make him take them all back, but he whinged so much she relented.

Friday October 20th

It's been in the news that Fergie's book has had a surprise surge in sales. Mum and Dad went a bit quiet when they heard that ...

I'm beginning to wish Dad had never put crayon to paper.

Saturday October 21st

Dad's a bit embarrassed, I think. He's been hurling darts at his Alex Ferguson dartboard with a vastly increased sense of purpose and vigour.

Sunday October 22nd

We're off to a book signing on Saturday. In the light of recent events, my heart is filled with a sense of terrible foreboding ...

Monday October 23rd

Dad's spent all day practising his autograph. It makes my head hurt just watching the look of concentration on his face.

Tuesday October 24th

Apparently it's been five years since The Spice Girls formed. Mum and Dad shared a glass of champagne to celebrate, and put on a few Spice Girls records. The feelings it set off in me, dear diary. The fear that was struck into my very being when I heard the voice of Ginger Spice in the days before she was cast out into the darkness; and oh, the boom-titty-boom of my little heart as I heard the glorious Baby Spice suggest that a little zig-a-zigging might be on the cards. It was a deeply emotional moment.

It was a pretty emotional moment for Mum as well, I think. She got a bit squiffy and started saying in an icky kind of voice, 'Who's my beautiful little boy, then.' I was just on the point of accepting the compliment in my modest way, when I realised she was talking to Dad.

I felt a bit left out, to be honest ...

Wednesday October 25th

Dad's still practising his autograph. I hope someone turns up to this pesky book signing – I'd hate all this dedicated study to be in vain.

Thursday October 26th

Oh no, Dad's pen has run out of ink. He's got his eyes on my crayons again ...

Friday October 27th

Keep yer hands off, mate! I need these crayons to sustain my artistic outlet.

Dad's big day tomorrow; Mum and I get

to go along. This had better be a success. I shan't react kindly to an unsuccessful book signing, y'know …

Saturday October 28th

Zowee! Now that's what I call a reaction. You'll excuse me if I'm a bit too pooped to fill you in today …

Sunday October 29th

Eight thousand fans! Eight thousand! That's a lorra, lorra fans … Sometimes it's easy to underestimate just how popular I am. OK, so admittedly some of them probably turned up to see Dad, but I can't help thinking that I was the star of the show. And Dad didn't even embarrass me too much. He managed to sign all the books he was given very neatly, he didn't wear a skirt, and he didn't speak too much, which is always a fairly effective damage-limitation technique.

All in all, a rip-roaring success. Dad sold tons of books, spreading the Gospel According to Becks far and wide. Good thing too – it's Halloween on Tuesday. Who knows what terrible tricks the Big Bad Evil Ginger One will have up her sleeve …

Monday October 30th

Mum and Dad have plans to take me out trick or treating. This is the best idea they've had in ages. Word must have got back to Ginger Spice about my campaign to free the world from her evil tyranny. If she's gonna try and stop me, Halloween will be the perfect time, when her powers are at their peak.

But she hasn't reckoned on the skill, wit, canniness and ferocious intelligence of the Beckham household. It's a good thing we keep it under wraps, otherwise I might be in danger …

Tuesday October 31st

D-day. Tonight we must move with all the skill and precision of a military operation. I hate to doubt the integrity of Phoenix Chi, but I can't help feeling that she might have given the Ginger One the low-down on the layout of Beckingham Palace. Still, with our elaborate disguises and constant vigilance we shall be able to foil even her most dastardly plans. OK, so it's gonna take some pretty heavy disguising to stop my handsomeness shining through whatever costume Mum's got sorted out for me, but I have every faith in her.

Wish me luck, dear diary – we're going over …

NOVEMBER
2000

Wednesday November 1st

Phew! I'm pleased to report that Beckingham Palace remains, to the best of my knowledge, an Evil Ginger One-free zone. Not only that, but we got a pretty hefty trick or treating haul:

£3.63 *(Pesky skinflints! How's that supposed to keep me in the style to which I've become accustomed? Our neighbours had better sort their acts out.)*
1 old slipper *(Got thrown at us from out*

of a window. Frankly, I'm not sure why we kept hold of it – it doesn't contain a shred of cashmere ...)

1 bag Jelly Babies (*Dad's favourite – he scoffed the lot before we got home.*)

1 old humbug (*No, I'm not talking about Mum ...*)

3lbs rancid tomatoes (*Dad got a bit confused, unfortunately. He didn't quite twig that they were meant to be used in case we needed to play a trick on anyone; Mum went a bit green when he served them up as a late supper ...*)

Thursday November 2nd

Hmmm ... Thinking about it, our trick or treating haul wasn't that impressive. Maybe Mum was a bit too convincing as the Wicked Old Witch. Come to think of it, she didn't even dress up. Should I be worried?

Dad's a bit worried because England have got a new manager. He came home from football practice today and when Mum asked him what the name of the new sucker was, he said he couldn't remember, but that it was something like Olaf. It was on the telly later on that the dude's name is Sven Eriksson, and there was a whole load of hullaballo about whether he should have got the gig. Personally I think it's rather irresponsible of the powers that be. They're perfectly well aware that they pay their footballers for their feet, not for – how can I put this? – their little grey cells. How on earth are they supposed to remember a name like that?

Dad's doubly upset, actually. The new bloke's a Swede, and Dad hates swede.

Friday November 3rd

Ah, the tangled webs we weave. Mum and Dad are in a right old strop because all of the Manchester United football team have been invited to a Robbie Williams concert – except them. The reason? Apparently the Big Bad Evil Ginger One's going to be there, and people are worried that she and Mum might get into a fight.

Personally, I'm breathing a sigh of relief. I know Mum can be pretty terrifying sometimes (I wet my nappy this morning, just after she'd furnished me with a clean one – you shoulda seen her ...), but she's really no match for the Evil One when it comes to one-on-one combat. Mum's fuming, of course, but I think it's all for the best. Even though the Ginger One's popularity seems to be on the up, the time for a showdown hasn't come yet ...

Saturday November 4th

Bonfire night tomorrow. Mum said we're going to have a firework display in the garden, but to be honest I'm a bit worried about it. Dad has enough trouble lighting a candle, let alone putting on a fiery display of pyrotechnics ...

Sunday November 5th

Mum sent Dad out to buy a Catherine wheel this morning; he was out for ages, but came back completely empty-handed. He told Mum that he couldn't find anyone by that name, so Mum put on her own little fiery display of pyrotechnics. I'll say one thing for my ma – she's got a pair of lungs on her ...

So the plan's changed, and we're all going along to a firework party at the house of their friend John Elton – much more sensible all round, if you ask me ...

Monday November 6th

Ah, the music! Ah, the dancing! Ah, the ...

strange men! Boy oh boy, that was a party to remember. John Elton's a funny old stick – still insists on being called by his last name, and *very* friendly with Dad. Mum tried to hide her irritation, but I know her better than most: she was clearly a bit irked. He seemed pretty taken with yours truly, as well:

> **John Elton**: *Oooh, what a lovely little boy you are!*
> **Brooklyn**: *C'mon, pal, less of the little boy speak. We're both men of the world – let's talk chicks …*

He didn't seem very keen with that suggestion unfortunately, and went off to mingle. I could've sworn I saw him pat Dad's bottom one point – still, if the old boy's gonna dress like he does, he'll have to learn to take the consequences …

Tuesday November 7th

Zowee! They're making a TV documentary all about my dad. I've no doubt I shall be called upon to play a starring role; the thespian fire burns strongly within me, so I feel confident I shall shine on-screen. Just so long as Dad doesn't play up ...

Wednesday November 8th

Come to think of it, I have a sneaking suspicion that his antics can only make me appear in a favourable light. He can be my straight man – I'm the cat that's gonna give the public what they want ...

Thursday November 9th

Day one of filming tomorrow. Lights, camera ...

Friday November 10th

... action! Today's oeuvre centred around shots of Dad playing footy in the garden. It all went quite well until he got viciously tackled by one of the garden gnomes. Still, all's fair in love and football – it didn't justify the atrocious behaviour that followed. He lay on the ground feigning injury, and then kicked out and cracked the offending gnome's leg. I've got to be honest, dear diary – my personal prejudice aside, it was a shocking display. The referee, Larry the pottery Leprechaun, had no option but to award a red card. Dad really shouldn't have got so upset with him – his language was beyond the pale.

The camera team looked a bit bemused when all this was happening – I don't really blame them, unused as they are to the idiosyncrasies of my world. They're coming back on Sunday to film some more – hopefully Dad will have calmed down by then …

Saturday November 11th

Mum made a very helpful suggestion today. 'Why don't you play a nice game of peek-a-boo with Brooklyn for the cameras tomorrow, David? You're good at that, aren't you?'

Dad looked dead pleased – I think he'd been worrying about his next celluloid experience. We've been practising all day.

Sunday November 12th

BROOKLYN VS DAD PEEK-A-BOO
MATCH – LATE RESULTS

Brooklyn 10, Dad 0

It's not that I don't like winning, you understand, but Dad *keeps* forgetting what to say. The documentary director was very good – he said, 'Why don't we come back tomorrow and film you in the kitchen? Your wife says you're a very good chef ...'

Ah well, he asked for it ...

Monday November 13th

Oh my gawd, it gets worse every day. Dad decided he was going to cook a Lentil Bake for the film cameras. It started off OK, but all of a sudden he disappeared. After half an hour, the director told one of the crew to go and look for him, and the bloke found Dad lying in the bath looking at his watch.

Everyone looked a bit wild-eyed when Dad explained that the instructions on the packet of lentils said 'Soak in cold water for an hour.'

I hope they didn't get it all on film.

Tuesday November 14th

A day off from the rigours of filming. This whole thing isn't going at all how I planned; I think I'll try and keep out of the way from here on in.

Wednesday November 15th

Ignominy! Humiliation! Dad spent ages today giving the cameras a guided tour of his wardrobe. It was only when Mum got home that he realised it was her wardrobe they were looking at.

The camera team scarpered. I don't think we'll be seeing them again …

Thursday November 16th

And so my opportunity to become a TV star is scuppered, for now – unless they use the peek-a-boo footage. Frankly, I hope they don't; I'm really not the kinda guy who wants to make himself look great simply by juxtaposition to somebody with the IQ of a pickled egg.

We're being sent a rough cut of the documentary tomorrow. I don't think I'll have the courage to watch it.

Friday November 17th

Cor, what a palaver! Mum went completely doolally when she saw the documentary. Personally, I couldn't even be in the same room; but I was around when Mum called the director to tell him that he'd gone out of his way to make Dad look stupid, and that he'd have to cut out any bits that make him seem dim.

From the length of the conversation, I'd say that the director put up a pretty brave fight, but frankly he didn't stand a chance against Mum on the warpath. I did have some sympathy with him, though. It'd take a talented filmmaker indeed to make Dad look like Einstein; and if they cut out all the bits of him looking one sandwich short of a picnic, they're gonna end up with a very short show indeed …

I think it's best we put the whole affair behind us …

Saturday November 18th

Oh, a proud day in the Beckham household! How my heart bursts with love for my talented daddy.

Yes, call me fickle, but the calamities of the past few days have been forgotten; Dad has been returned to his lofty pedestal. Why? Because my pop, he from whose loins I am derived, is gonna captain the England footy side! 'Ere we go, 'ere we go, 'ere we go! We play Italy tonight, with skipper Becks at the helm …

Sunday November 19th

OK, OK, so we didn't, erm, we didn't *win*, exactly, but the lad's got to start somewhere. I'm not gonna let a little thing like a one-nil defeat get in the way of my pride and admiration for my daddio.

Monday November 20th

If he doesn't take me shopping soon to replenish my fast-depleting wardrobe, now *that* might get in the way of my pride and admiration …

   D'ya get the hint, Dad?

Tuesday November 21st

What a good boy he is. Clearly my sartorial dissatisfaction has shined though. Brooklyn and Cap'n Becks hit the shops tomorrow. Look out Barclaycard, here we come …

Wednesday November 22nd

Now that is what I call a shopping spree.
Unfortunately, all that retail therapy takes it
out of a kid – I'll have to fill you in on the
day's purchases tomorrow.

Thursday November 23rd

DAD'S SHOPPING LIST

Togs, obviously. *Funky little numbers
from Gucci, Prada etc. I had to bawl a
bit when he tried to sneak into
Knickerbox, but apart from that he was
pretty well behaved.*

**A few copies of David Beckham: My
World.** *After all, sales are sales.*

Car polish and chamois leathers. *The
motors are still stuck out in the driveway
getting dirtier by the day, as the garage is
still chocka with boxes of records and*

books. *Dunno what he intends to do with them, but he'd better get a move on.*

1 packet of Jammie Dodgers. *(He hadn't had any since breakfast.)*

Flowers for Mum. *She was a bit miffed when we left this morning because Dad forgot to put sugar in her tea. It wouldn't have been so bad, only he forgot to put milk in as well. And tea, unfortunately. But the hot water was expertly boiled, so I think Mum may have been overreacting.*

BROOKLYN'S SHOPPING LIST

Togs, obviously. *One of the great things about being a growing lad is that I'm constantly growing out of my gear, which means a high replacement turnover. What Mum and Dad's excuse for their high replacement turnover is, I'm not quite sure, but long may it* continue if it means I get to hit the boutiques with them.

Nappies. *Tried to play that one down a bit. I've got to say, I think it's high time Mum ditched the diapers. I seem to have a pretty good control over the old waterworks now …*

Sweets! *Can't get enough of 'em. One of the exquisite joys of moving on to solid foodstuffs is the infinite variety of confection available to me. Chocolate, sherbet, little fruity chews – this, dear diary, is* haute cuisine *from where I'm standing. If I can only work out a way of keeping Dad's dirty little mitts off my Jelly Babies, I shall be a true sweetmeat* gourmand …

Friday November 24th

Oh dear, more problems chez Beckham. Mum's banned Dad from going on such elaborate shopping sprees. Now, I don't want to accuse the pot of calling the kettle black or anything, but let us not forget that Mum has over two hundred pairs of high heels. Dad's only got two. A slight discrepancy, methinks …

Saturday November 25th

Cor, she means business. She's got Dad to agree to cut down his spending to incorporate just three new pairs of Armani jeans a week …

Sunday November 26th

How's the guy gonna manage? He'll be reduced to the status of an ordinary person!

Monday November 27th

I really think Mum's cutting off her nose to spite her face. I can hardly see her relishing the thought of being seen about town with a scruffy hubby …

Tuesday November 28th

… and if Dad has to, I can hardly bring myself to say it, re-use his clothes, it only means more washing for Mum. Not that I want to perpetuate outdated gender stereotypes, you understand – but you remember what happened last time Dad tried to wash his football kit. The oven's never recovered …

Wednesday November 29th

What a charmer! Dad sure knows how to get round Mum, if nothing else. Knowing how much she loves his tattoos (there's no accounting for taste, dear diary – that much my short life has already taught me …) he's told her he's gonna get another one.

A skilful deflection of the shopping-ban issue worthy of an England skipper, if you ask me.

Thursday November 30th

Not that I actually approve of Dad's tattoo addiction, you understand. Let us not forget that he's got the word 'Brooklyn' tattooed where the sun don't shine. I've live in constant fear of the day he tries to get me to have a similar 'Dad' tattoo in the same place.

If I've told you once, I've told you a thousand times, Daddio – this lily-white butt remains tattoo-free, d'ya hear?

I just hope Dad doesn't go over the top this time, but quite where I inherit my mindless optimism from, I'm not sure.

It's not long till Christmas now. I'd better get scrawling to my old pal Santa with this year's Xmas requirements …

DECEMBER
2000

Friday December 1st

Dear Santa

Sorry to trouble you at this busy time of year, but I thought I'd better drop you a line to discuss my requirements for the forthcoming festive season. Perhaps you could pop one of your deputy elves in the driving seat whilst you attend to my needs.

I think it might be best if I gave you a rough idea of what I don't want for

Christmas. I presume Mum and Dad have been in discussion with you, but they have some pretty funny ideas sometimes, and I don't want them to get the wrong end of the stick. Firstly, I'd like to put a total ban on copies of Dad's book and Mum's record. I've heard them plotting that they'll be giving this stuff out for Christmas, but I know the truth about the merchandise in the garage – copies of Fergie's book are out for the same reason, if you don't mind.

Secondly, let's steer clear of the cuddly toys, shall we? The furry population of my bedroom is fast approaching unsustainable levels, and we don't want a demographic crisis on our hands.

Finally, and most importantly, nothing purple. Trust me on this, Santa – I know Mum's gonna be relentless in her campaign to thrust me into some ridiculous purple togs, so let's not give her any ammunition, huh?

Outside those parameters, I'm pretty unfussy. Sweets are good – I've recently developed a taste for them (especially the nice chocolaty ones that make a real mess); toys are always a good option, as long as they make plenty of noise and are suitable for being mischievously left underfoot; and bearing in mind the limitations set out above, keep the togs coming. Liaise with Dad on that one, could you? Generally he has pretty good taste, but don't let him get carried away with a) skirts, b) ladies' underwear and c) bandannas. He'll try and persuade you, but don't listen.

Thanks in advance – I'll drop you a line when you deliver the booty.

Yours etc

Brooklyn

PS Have you given any thought to updating your Santa costume? I think you should – it's so last century …

Saturday December 2nd

I hope Santa didn't mind my fashion tip at the end of the letter. It wasn't meant to be insulting, just helpful. When you're as stylish as me, the responsibility to let others reap the benefit of your sartorial judgement is immense, and people don't always take it the right way.

Ah well, if I wake up to a lump of coal in my stocking on Xmas morn, I'll know to keep my trap shut in the future.

Sunday December 3rd

Dad's serious about the extra tattoo. It's going to be on his arm, and it's going to be in another language. This is asking for trouble – you'd think he'd master English before fine-tuning his advanced translation skills.

Monday December 4th

Mum's thrilled. He's going to get the word Victoria tattooed on his arm in a different language. I can see why she's so chuffed – I'd have been tickled pink if Dad had had the foresight to have his Brooklyn tattoo emblazoned over his bum in, say, Swahili – that way I wouldn't have been such a laughing stock.

Ah well, it seems the boy's learning, slowly but surely. Well, slowly certainly. They're off to an Indian restaurant tonight to check out the Hindi.

Tuesday December 5th

Do you ever get a sense of impending disaster? I can't help thinking that Dad's going to get all confused and have 'Prawn Vindaloo' irreplaceably etched on his arm. He's off to the tattooist tomorrow.

Wednesday December 6th

Well, he's gone and done it. Just looks like a load of old scribbles to me, but it seems to have done the business with Mum – she's all over him. I wish I knew if he'd spelled everything correctly. At least if it's all wrong, I'd have time to prepare myself.

Thursday December 7th

Mum's terribly inconsistent these days. Having taken note of the devastating effect Dad's latest accessory has had on her, I took to wondering whether I should follow suit in order to get Baby Spice in a similar state of mindless devotion. So I got a black pen and used it to draw a similar pattern on my arm. If you think she took that badly, you should have seen her reaction when she noticed the practice scrawls all over the wallpaper. Talk about going ballistic – she's been a-huffin' and a-puffin' all day.

Don't worry, Dad! I won't tell her that the wallpaper scrawls are yours. But stop pinching my crayons to do it, huh? Otherwise I might just have to change my mind …

Friday December 8th

Doh! It's been in the paper that some egghead has noticed that – you guessed it – Dad's spelled 'Victoria' wrong in Hindi. Apparently, two letters have been mis-written.

To me, this whole affair is an interesting distillation of the problems of celebrity. Not only does one's every move (and the every move of one's parents) get intimately reported day by day, but even worse, they get it so wrong. OK, so Dad spelled two letters wrong, but that's completely missing the point. I don't notice those journos concentrating on how many letters he got *right*, now do I? Frankly, I think that the lad's done pretty well. A few weeks ago, before practising for his book signings, he had trouble spelling his own name, let alone Mum's.

Sorry if I sound put out, dear diary, but as I watch Dad's intellectual development largely mirror my own, I feel strongly that nothing should be done to discourage him ...

Saturday December 9th

Mum and Dad are concentrating very hard on writing their Christmas cards. I think I'd better do the same ...

Sunday December 10th

Yo Phoenix

At this festive time of the year, when we offer peace and good will to all men, women and toddlers, I thought it would be a kindly gesture for me to offer the hand of friendship, despite your recent foul defection to the camp of she whose name with which it would be inappropriate to sully a Christmas card.

C'mon, Phoenix babe! You know I need an ally in this terrible battle against her insidious rule. You know my door is always open for you (just have a word with the security dudes at the front gate). Together we can bring meaning and order to the world...

B

Dear Phoenix Chi

Happy Christmas

Respect

from

Brooklyn

Monday December 11th

Hey, Baby

So, Christmas – we're talking intimate little lovers' gifts, romantic cuddles by the Christmas tree, and, yep, you guessed it, mistletoe. And you know my mum and dad – they don't do these things by halves. When they get the mistletoe in, they get the mistletoe in – lorry loads of the stuff, if you take my meaning. Bottom line is, I'll be expecting at least one kiss under each and every sprig from those perfect little cherry-reds of yours. You'd better put a few hours aside for the whole operation, because I don't intend to let you off lightly.

B xxx

Dear Baby Spice

Happy Christmas

With all my love
(and I think you know what
I'm talking about...)

Brooklyn

Tuesday December 12th

I've been in two minds about whether to draft a Christmas card for Mum and Dad. On balance, I think it will be a bit safer to keep our relationship on the slightly restricted vocal basis that we've established hitherto. I don't want to freak them out by revealing my linguistic virtuosity just yet. And I don't want to make Dad jealous.

Wednesday December 13th

Aaaaaaarrrrgggggghhhhhhh!!!!!!! Mum and Dad were discussing whether they should be sending a Christmas card to the Big Bad Evil Ginger One today. C'mon guys, a bit of solidarity if you please! Don't tell me that you're going down the path that Phoenix Chi so unwisely followed.

Thursday December 14th

Mum and Dad are talking about what they both want for Christmas. This was a deeply alarming conversation. Dad was moderately restrained – the usual suggestions of new clothes and fast cars. This I can handle. But Mum, woe is me, suggested that she might quite like a new recording studio built in the house.

Even Dad looked a bit shell-shocked, and not without reason. Mum was singing in the shower just yesterday morning and it sounded like the plumbing had gone up the spout. I hope he doesn't crack under the pressure and give her what she wants …

Friday December 15th

Yikes! It's a good thing I'm around to sort things out, otherwise this has the potential to turn into a pretty disastrous Christmas.

Mum and Dad were talking earlier on

about what exactly they were going to get their little bundle of joy (that's me, in case you were wondering) for Christmas. They have these grand plans to turn my bedroom into some sort of astronomical theme park – a big dome with replica stars and stuff. What do I want with replica stars – I've got two real ones in the house already, and they provide quite enough work as it is, thanks awfully. I'd better get in touch with Father Christmas again – I reckon he's got a pretty good head on his shoulders. He'll know what to do.

Saturday December 16th

Dear Father Christmas

I'm really sorry to be pestering you this close to the big day. I know you must be kinda busy, servicing your sleigh, making sure Rudolf's in good form. If it would help, I'm sure Dad would lend you his Ferrari to help you get around when you're over this way – it's pretty nippy, and – to be honest – it would be a relief to get it out of the driveway.

Anyway, the reason for my letter is pretty serious, otherwise I wouldn't bug you. Problem is, Mum and Dad seem set on some kind of flight-of-fancy building work for my bedroom as a Chrissy present. Now, I don't want to sound ungrateful or anything, but home improvements weren't really what I had in mind. I know the Oldies mean well, but it would be a terrible disappointment to a kid if he didn't have anything to unwrap on Christmas Day.

Do you think you could have a word with them? I'd really appreciate it.

Hope to catch you on the 25th.

All the best
Brooklyn

PS Don't take what I said in my last letter about your Santa outfit too seriously. The more I think about it, the more I come to the conclusion that it's a classic design. Sure, not many people can pull it off – but if anyone can, you're the dude.

PPS I've got this nasty feeling that Dad's going to succumb to Mum's request for a recording studio. Is there anything you can do to stop this terrible idea? If not, any chance of a pair of earplugs in my stocking?

Sunday December 17th

Mum and Dad are still plugging away at their Christmas cards. I know they've got a lot of the things, but you'd think that they were trying to write *War and Peace*. They've got a little system going – Mum writes the card, and Dad signs it with his thumbprint and puts it in the envelope. He did start out trying to sign his real name, but they decided that they wanted to get all the cards out for *this* Christmas, so they changed tack.

Monday December 18th

I'm sure they're supposed to be writing something on the envelope too. Ah well, what do I know? I'm just a kid …

Tuesday December 19th

On second thoughts, sometimes I feel like old Father Time around these two. They've finally finished their mammoth task but I'm still convinced there's something missing. Even Mum and Dad look a bit concerned. They've been staring at the blank envelopes all day, scratching their heads. Dad said, 'I know, I'll call Alex and ask him if there's anything else we should be doing with these,' but Mum went a bit prickly and told him she had everything under control. She didn't look too confident, though …

Wednesday December 20th

Stamps! Good old Mum! It's taken her a while, but she got there in the end. She's had Dad licking stamps and putting them on the blank envelopes all morning. Dad had a bit of a moan, but she told him that she couldn't possibly do it, as stamps contain at least one calorie per lick. That said, she went and watched telly with a tin of rice pudding.

On balance, I think it's good that she gives Dad these little tasks to do. He made a good job of it, too, just as soon as he'd worked out which side of the stamp he was supposed to lick.

Thursday December 21st

Well, the cards have all gone off. I still can't help thinking that there was something missing off the envelopes, but I've got to have faith in my parents' savvy.

Depressing, isn't it?

Friday December 22nd

Three days till Chrissy. I can't help but admit that I'm getting a bit excited. Dad put our Christmas tree up today and I spent a very satisfactory afternoon pulling off some of the lower branches. Mum didn't seem to share my enjoyment of the whole operation, though. I hope the old Christmas spirit descends on her soon.

Saturday December 23rd

Two days! I hope Father Christmas got my letter. Mum and Dad have been a bit quiet about the whole issue of the presents, although Mum's still dropping hints about the recording studio.

On second thoughts, maybe it wouldn't be such a bad thing. At least it'd be soundproofed. I'm sick and tired of her morning sing-song curdling the milk in my porridge.

Sunday December 24th

Baby Spice came round for a Christmas drink this evening. I'm inordinately pleased to report that her appetite for kissing yours truly under the mistletoe seemed absolutely insatiable. She gave me a little present, which she put under the tree; I was a bit embarrassed not to have anything to give her in return, but I suppose it can't hurt if I'm seen to be playing a bit hard-to-get …

I wonder if Santa will pop in for a chinwag tonight. Maybe I'll try and stay awakezzzzzzz …

Monday December 25th

Happy Christmas!!!! Good old Mum and Dad, they know how to make a festive day of it. Dad was dead excited when he woke up, but Mum told him that he wasn't allowed to open any of his presents whilst he was still in his pyjamas. Ordinarily I'd think that that was a bit bossy, but it did prolong the excitement.

The prezzie haul was pretty impressive. Clearly my letter had got through to Father Christmas (not a peep from him last night, incidentally – that dude knows how to work quietly …) so Mum and Dad had been tipped off that I'd require a few decent trinkets to unwrap under the tree:

BROOKLYN'S XMAS TRINKETS
1 copy David Beckham: My World – *surprise, surprise. Clearly Santa had overlooked my little stipulation.*
Sweets, sweets, sweets, sweets, sweets! *Santa more than made up for the above-mentioned faux-pas with this. I've got*

every sweetie you care to name. Even better, Mum bought Dad a whole load of Smarties and Jammie Dodgers, so hopefully he'll keep his hands off my goodies.

The usual haul of Versace, Armani, Prada and Gucci – *and that's just my range of designer nappies. Trust me, the Oldies have excelled themselves. They must want something, but that's cool with me – bribery will get you everywhere ...*

Mum even seemed quite pleased with the karaoke machine Dad bought her. She seemed a bit alarmed that he'd had it installed in a titanium-lined studio at the bottom of the garden, way out of earshot, with walls about eight-feet thick; but if she suspected that Dad's intentions were at all untoward, she didn't show it.

But the best part of the day was lunch! Boy oh boy, did I gorge. Turkey, stuffing, the works. Dad was going to do the cooking, but Mum suggested that he should sit down and write his thank you letters instead, which was a pretty deft move on her part, if you ask me – that should keep him quiet till Easter. It was touch-and-go for a bit when Dad wouldn't take off the paper hat he got from his Christmas cracker – he clearly thought that it was a pretty zappy piece of headwear – but I did see him hide it away in the drawer in his bedroom. That boy will put anything on his head …

Yep, all in all a successful Christmas Day. I know we sometimes have our differences, but I wouldn't change the Beckham family trio for anything.

Tuesday December 26th

Cold turkey for lunch. I love this turkey

stuff – I could eat it till the cows come home. In fact, I could eat it till the cows come home, have dinner, turn in for the night, and then leave again for work the next morning. Lemme at it …

Wednesday December 27th

Turkey sandwiches. Yum, yum …

Thursday December 28th

Maybe I spoke too soon. This turkey stuff's all very well, but I'm beginning to hanker after a bit of a change. So's Dad, by all accounts. He suggested to Mum that we might have something a bit different, and she said, 'Fine, you cook then!' before popping out to torture her vocal cords at the bottom of the garden.

Sure enough, we had turkey for dinner.

Friday December 29th

I'm gonna turn into a bleedin' turkey if I'm not careful …

Saturday December 30th

I knew it! I absolutely, one hundred per cent, knew it! Mum and Dad have appeared in a list of the top five most glamorous people in the country. No surprise there (although whoever wrote the list might think differently if they knew things about them that I know). But – and here's the catch – also in the list is a lady called Ffion Hague. No immediate problem there, perhaps, but have you seen her hubby? Bald as a coot and with all the street cred of one of my old nappies. You see, Dad! Give yourself these ridiculous haircuts, and people are gonna compare you to ridiculous people! When are you gonna start believing that I know what I'm talkin' about?

JANUARY
2001

Monday January 1st

Well, OK!!!! Things are hotting up! Things are looking good! Things are ... oh, I'll just get on with it, shall I?

Mum wants to buy a big ol' house in London. This is the best news I've heard all year. OK, so it's the *only* news I've heard all year, but it's gonna take some beating. There's nothing wrong with Beckingham Palace, you understand – it's a perfect country pad. But it is a bit out in the sticks. A cat like me needs a base in the bright lights of the big city in order to be the ultimate society animal. Actually, I'm a bit surprised it's taken her this long to come round to my way of thinking. Let's just hope it's not another whim …

Tuesday January 2nd

Oooohhh! Handbags at dawn. Mum wants to buy the same house as Mrs Madonna. It's in a place called Notting Hill, and it's, ahem, mucho swankio, if you get my drift.

C'mon Madge, babe, you're a woman of the world. Let's not make a battle out of this, huh? You know better than to take on the *savoir faire* and intellectual might of the Beckham household …

Wednesday January 3rd

… on second thoughts, I hope Mum hasn't set her heart on it. She doesn't take disappointment at all well.

Thursday January 4th

Of course, the obvious solution is some kind of house-share scheme. With their busy schedules, Mrs Madonna and the Oldies are hardly likely to run into each other too often; and it would have the added advantage of me being able to re-kindle the fire of my relationship with the luscious Lourdes.

I don't want you to think I'm being fickle, dear diary – Baby Spice is still the only one for me. But hey, even though I'm coming up for the ripe old age of two, I'm still a bit of a spring chick in the grand scheme of things. I've gotta play the field a bit, if only to validate the lifestyle choices I've already made. How can I explain this simply? If I hadn't, for example, spent time rigorously sampling the delights of confection available to me, I wouldn't know that I'd rank Jelly Babies far above Chocolate Buttons and

Sherbert Dips, now would I? The same thing with my darling Baby. How can I prove to myself that my love for her is the pure and wonderful thing I think it is, if I've nothing to compare her with?

Heh, heh! Now I've justified that to myself – look out ladies, here comes Brooklyn ...

Friday January 5th

I TAKE IT BACK!!!! I TAKE IT ALL BACK!!!! LOURDES, I NEVER WANT TO SEE YOU AGAIN. I NEVER WANT TO SEE *ANYONE* AGAIN. EXCUSE ME WHILST I EMIGRATE TO KATMANDU ...

Saturday January 6th

I'm sooooooo embarrassed. In fact, embarrassed doesn't even come close. Mum and Dad have just said in public that they would pose naked in *Playboy* if they thought it was the right thing to do.

Sunday January 7th

Now listen dudes, and listen good. It's not the right thing to do. Did you hear that? No? Allow me to reiterate: IT'S NOT THE RIGHT THING TO DO! IT'S THE WRONG THING TO DO! WRONG, WRONG, WRONG! D'YA HEAR?

Monday January 8th

I could cry with frustration. In fact, I think I will cry with frustration. Excuse me for a minute.

Waaaaahhhhhh!!!!!!!!!!

Tuesday January 9th

Picture the scene. Just picture it. The photographer says, 'Ah, Mr Beckham, just pop your clothes on the chair there, would you? That's lovely. Ooooh, what a dashing little thong that is – I must just get a quick snap of that!' All of a sudden several squillion people see Mum and Dad in the buff and the secret of Dad's, er, gender-defying dresswear will become a matter of public record. You'd think Mum would want to put the kibosh on it, but as far as I can tell it was her bleedin' idea.

It's all terribly confusing. I've noticed that Mum has become rather plumper in the old milk supply department, and it is true that Dad seems to be inexplicably appreciative of it all; but seeing as how she's so concerned about shedding the pounds, you'd think she'd at least try and go down a coupla cup sizes before parading for the camera in her birthday suit.

All I can do is rely on their common sense prevailing.

You can see why I'm so worried …

Wednesday January 10th

This is turning into a really rotten year. It's not like they need the dough. It's not like they can't put bread on the table. If it came to that, it'd be much better for them to, er, knead the dough rather than go to such humiliating extremes. Maybe I'm misreading the situation. Maybe we're in a dire financial situation that has caused my dear parents to consider such hare-brained schemes in order to keep me in expensive toys.

Thursday January 11th

A terrible thought has just crossed my brain. Maybe [gulp!] we're down to our last couple of million …

Friday January 12th

The horror! It's too much to consider. How will we live?

Saturday January 13th

I'm gonna have to take the bull by the horns. It won't be easy, but I'm willing to do my bit in this horrific family catastrophe. What if I cut my clothes bill in half? That should reduce our annual outgoings by at least fifty grand.

Sunday January 14th

But what's fifty grand these days? Hell, it won't even buy me the five-gear, four-cylinder Aston Martin baby buggy I've got my eyes on for my birthday. We're gonna have to find other ways to cut down.

Monday January 15th

Haircuts! As a family, we could definitely cut down on the haircuts. You see, every cloud has a silver lining.

Tuesday January 16th

Hmmm … Maybe the haircut idea isn't such a good one. You know my mum and dad – they always take things to extremes. The 'boiled egg' look is ghastly, I know, but at least I've had time to get used to it. And imagine if they decided to go hippy – it'd be so last century.

Wednesday January 17th

Nope. I'm just not cut out for budgeting. If they can't bring home the bacon, they're just gonna have to find other ways of earning a crust. But, and this is a stipulation which I'm gonna have to insist on, they've got to do it with their clothes on!!!!!!

Thursday January 18th

Dad's up for a pay review tomorrow. There's light at the end of the tunnel. He'd better be on his best behaviour …

Friday January 19th

NOW THAT'S WHAT I CALL A RESULT! Dad's gonna earn a cool hundred grand. A week!!! Lets put that into some sort of context. At 1p a Jelly Baby, we're talking a million Jelly Babies a week. Of course, I reckon I could negotiate some kind of bulk discount, but that's a good working figure.

Not that I need a million Jelly Babies a week, of course. About half that would probably do, provided Dad gets his own supply and keeps his hands off mine.

Saturday January 20th

I hope you don't think I seem untowardly interested in my Dad's earning power, dear diary, but I have gotta think about my future …

Still, if you think *I'm* bad, you should see the Oldies. They've been running round the front room whooping for joy for 48 hours now. It's very exhausting.

Sunday January 21st

Sunday. The day of rest. I wish Mum and Dad would give it a rest.

Monday January 22nd

Wahey! Now this is getting serious. Dad's just been offered a million quid to sponsor some poncy sunglasses. A million quid! All he's gotta do is have a few snaps taken and all of a sudden he's earned himself ten weeks' pay. Bob's yer uncle. Well, he's not *my* uncle, obviously, but you get my drift.

For someone with the intellectual capacity of a doughnut, that boy can earn.

Tuesday January 23rd

We're going to have trouble spending all this dosh. I didn't say we couldn't do it, mind – but it's gonna be tough …

Wednesday January 24th

Hopefully this sudden influx of cash-o-roonie will put paid to their daft ideas about getting their kit off for all and sundry. I had this horrible premonition that they would suddenly get me in on the act. Lemme get this straight – I ain't the running-around-in-the-buff kinda toddler. 'Modesty' is my watchword. Along with 'style', 'hipness' and 'full nappy', but I prefer to keep the last one to myself.

Still, it's a narrow escape. Can you imagine what Phoenix Chi would have said? She's coming round tomorrow. I don't think I can bring myself to fill her in on my folks' latest idea …

Thursday January 25th

An interesting exchange:

Phoenix Chi: *Yo Brooklyn, gimme some skin. How's it hangin', dude?*

Brooklyn: *Oh, you know, PC – another day another dollar. Well, another million dollars, actually. And the rest. It's good to know one's pater is being offered the kind of recompense he really deserves.*

Phoenix Chi: *A million big ones? Last time they got that sort of dough in one hit was for their wedding snaps when you had to dress up in that purple skirt. What they doin' to ya this time, my friend?*

Brooklyn: *You had to bring it up, didn't you, PC?*

Phoenix Chi: *[Smirks]*

Brooklyn: *Since you ask, I got nothing to do with this particular gig. Dad's got to* *model some shades and that, it seems, is that.*

Phoenix Chi: *Well, if I were you, I'd read the small print.*

Brooklyn: *C'mon, PC, I'm only one. My, er, my reading's not quite up to scratch.*

Phoenix Chi: *Well, get your Dad to read it for you.*

Brooklyn: *Hmmm … I'm, er, I'm not sure his reading's quite up to it either, to be honest.*

Phoenix Chi: *Alright, already! Just do your research. You know what your folks are like. I don't want to see my man Brooklyn in fancy dress again. I got your best interests at heart …*

She's got a point. Whilst I think I'd look pretty hip in a natty pair of shades, I'd rather call the shots regarding where and when I wear them. Even a million bucks isn't worth a cat losing his freedom of decision for ...

Friday January 26th

Yesterday's conversation with PC rather painfully avoided the thorny subject of the BBEGO. I do hope she's beginning to see the light once more.

Saturday January 27th

I can't tell you how relieved I am that our financial situation is healthier than I thought. Only a few weeks now till birthday number two; the last bash was a pretty extravagant affair, befitting the importance of the occasion. I suspect the Oldies are gonna want to outdo themselves this time round, and it'll cost a pretty penny, you can be sure of that.

Good old Dad. You can't say he doesn't come up with the goods. It's been an action-packed few months for him – he's negotiated a lovely-jubbly pay rise and written a book. I hope Mum doesn't feel left out …

Sunday January 28th

Eeek! I spoke too soon!

It seems Mum's not content to let her hubby enter the heady world of serious literature all alone. What I'm trying to say is – Mum's decided to write a book as well!!!

I don't think I can face this. It's been stressful enough having one literary lion in the family. Now I've got to go through the whole thing again: the mental exertion, the long hours, the celebrity tantrums – and that's just Dad trying to tie his shoelaces. I'm really not sure Mum's cut out for a life of literature; I hope Dad talks her out of it.

Monday January 29th

Aw, Dad! A fat lot of good you are. He's been really encouraging – he even offered to help! Mum was very good and didn't laugh even a little bit.

I hope she's getting well paid for this.

Tuesday January 30th

Zowee!!!! I take it all back. Another million for the book. Y'know, a kid could get blasé about all these million-quid checks rolling in. As long as the old dear stays reasonably sensible, maybe this could be a successful project all round. Perhaps I should draw her up a list of subjects to avoid in order to prevent tears:

BROOKLYN'S LIST OF SUBJECTS MUM SHOULD AVOID IN HER BOOK.

1. Dad. *I know, I know, it sounds harsh, but*

every time she opens her mouth she says
something to embarrass him. Dad – I'm not
trying to take you outta the limelight,
honestly. You'll thank me for this.

2. Clothes. *OK, so I'm limiting her*
pretty extremely, but she can get awfully
dull when she starts banging on about
her wardrobe. (The real reason, of
course, is that I don't want her to start
talking about some of the nonsense she
dresses me up in, but let's keep that
between ourselves, shall we?)

3. Singing. *You call that singing?*

Hmmm … That doesn't give her a lot to
write about. I'm gonna have to give this
some thought.

Wednesday January 31st

BROOKLYN'S LIST OF THINGS THAT MUM SHOULD DEFINITELY WRITE ABOUT IN HER BOOK

1. **Brooklyn**. *Obvious, really.*
2. *Er, that's it …*

She's a lucky gal. With editorial control like mine, she can't lose!

FEBRUARY
2001

Thursday February 1st

Y'know, I'm beginning to give serious thought to writing a book myself. Sounds ridiculous, I know, but if Mum and Dad can do it, I don't see the problem. And it'd probably mean another million in the bank – seems to be the going rate.

But then, I guess I'd have to reveal to the world all my secret knowledge about Mum and Dad's antics. I know they drive me up the wall sometimes, but I do love 'em to bits really – I could never bring myself to let everyone know what they're actually like.

So no, my innermost thoughts remain unfit, I fear, for public consumption. It's probably best that way …

Friday February 2nd

My heart is a-flutter! I'm too besotted to write …

Saturday February 3rd

My love! Such a tender gesture. I am speechless with adoration!

Sunday February 4th

What more romantic gesture could the lovely Baby Spice make to signify her love for me?

She came round on Friday with an early birthday present for yours truly. I am now more convinced than ever that she is the true love of my life. So close to her heart am

I that she has bought me my very own star! Yep, twinkling somewhere up there is a star called Brooklyn Beckham. My place in history is assured.

The subtext is clear to me. I am *her* star; the light in her darkness; the heavenly body in the void of her life. (And yes, my body is heavenly, before you ask.)

My only problem is this: how can I reciprocate? It's comin' up to Valentine's Day and I'm gonna have to get my thinking cap on …

Monday February 5th

What do I get the Spice Girl who has everything? I know a kiss from my tender lips ought to be enough, but these chicks can be kinda materialistic. I'm going to have to come up with the goods.

Tuesday February 6th

Maybe I should ask Phoenix Chi. She and Scary Spice are coming round tomorrow for tea. I'm sure she'll have some good ideas, just as long as she hasn't been completely won over by the Big Bad Evil Ginger One …

Wednesday February 7th

Dah! Phoenix Chi's no good!

> **Brooklyn**: *Hey PC, I need some feminine advice.*
>
> **Phoenix Chi**: *Yeah, yeah, you guys. You can't put one foot in front of the other without the help of us chicks.*
>
> **Brooklyn**: *Whaddya sayin'? I didn't see you around when I started walking …*
>
> **Phoenix Chi**: *OK, OK! So what's the problem? Hit me with it.*

Brooklyn: *I need to know what to get Baby Spice for Valentine's Day.*

Phoenix Chi: *Aw, shucks, dude. I thought you'd got her out of your system.*

Brooklyn: *[Sighs]*

Phoenix Chi: *Dude?*

Brooklyn: *[Sighs again]*

Phoenix Chi: *DUDE?*

Brooklyn: *[Sighs a bit more, dreamily]*

Phoenix Chi: *DUDE! WAKE UP! YOU GOTTA GET A GRIP ON YOURSELF! SHE'S JUST A CHICK!*

Brooklyn: *She may be just a chick to you, PC, but to me she is everything.*

Phoenix Chi: *Hey, you got it bad, man. Well, can't you just get her a card like everyone else?*

Brooklyn: *Well that's just the problem. You know what she just bought me? My very own star. Pretty classy, huh?*

But to be honest, PC didn't have much in the way of suggestions. I'm going to have to rely on my own imagination and unflappably romantic nature.

Thursday February 8th

I've been toying with the idea of having another crack at a bit of poetry, but on balance I don't think it would be a very good idea. I tried it once before, when Baby first came into my life and I was barely a few tender months old. OK, so I've matured since then, but, though I say so myself, knowing my limitations is one of my strengths. I only have to look at Mum and Dad to see that, in spite of their attempts to prove me wrong, literature really isn't in my genes.

Friday February 9th

The only thing I know for sure that Baby

Spice wants is this thing called a Zigga-Zig-Aaaahhh. All the Spice Girls want one – they even wrote a song about it. Problem is, I ain't got the foggiest what it is.

I wonder if Mum's got one. She probably has. She seems to have most things.

Saturday February 10th

Spent the whole day snooping about the house looking for something that remotely resembles a Zigga-Zig-Aaaahhh, but no joy. Maybe I'll ask Mum tomorrow.

Sunday February 11th

Doh! Did my very best to formulate the following sentence: 'Say, Mum. Don't go askin' me no questions – this is on a strictly need-to-know basis – but I don't suppose you could point me in the direction of a Zigga-Zig-Aaahhh, could you?'

Unfortunately the last bit was all I could

manage, and Mum thought I was trying to sing one of her songs. She shoved the record on and started trying to get me to sing a duet with her. My poor old lugholes still haven't recovered.

Monday February 12th

Time is running out! I have a terrible suspicion that I'm not going to be able to do anything that shows Baby the true depth of my feelings for her. Soon enough we will drift apart, like ships that pass in the night

Tuesday February 13th

Who am I kidding? The poor girl's only human! Even if she doesn't hear from me tomorrow, she'll just assume I'm playing hard-to-get. The very notion of me not returning her love will be so terrible to her that her imagination will reject it utterly.

Phew! That was a close shave.

Wednesday February 14th

You know, a day like today could prove to be a serious blow to a kid's ego. Here I am, the most famous one-year-old on the planet, and for the second year running, how many Valentine's cards do I get? Yep, you guessed. Zero. Zilch. Zip. Not a single card – what is the world coming to?

With that unerring maternal instinct, Mum knew exactly what was wrong when I started to bawl my eyes out. 'Is ickle Brooklyn sad because he didn't get any Valentine's cards? Well, never mind. Nor did Daddy.'

She's not fooling me, though. I saw her standing by the gates when the postman turned up with three big sacks of cards; and I was watching as she had a quick rifle through and then chucked them all in the bin.

Dad's been looking a bit bemused about his lack of cards – but he knows better than to say anything about it. Clever boy …

Thursday February 15th

I'm still smarting about the fact that everyone's ignored me.

Friday February 16th

I have so much to give, yet I am ignored so wantonly. There'd better be some changes by next Valentine's Day, lemme tell ya. Excuse me whilst I go and sulk …

Saturday February 17th

Hey, this sulking thing gets results!

There I was, being thoroughly bad-tempered – crying, huffing, puffing; generally getting on Mum's nerves – when she comes up with an offer I can't refuse! She scooped me up in her arms and asked me if I want to sing on her next single!!!!!

As if the question even demands a response. Of course I wanna sing. It's about time I made my debut. It's very good of Mum to make me the offer – she must be pretty well aware that the chances are I'll be stealing the limelight from her – but that's motherly love for you. I'm going to have to get the old vocal cords into shape …

Sunday February 18th

Do Re Mi Fa Sol La Ti Do!

Mmmm … Nice!

Monday February 19th

Maybe I should be working on something a bit less classical, a bit hipper. Lemme think…

Tuesday February 20th

A-wop-bop-a-loo-bop-a-lop-bam-boom…

Now that's more like it! I could get use to this singing malarkey. I feel the rhythm surging through my veins.

Wednesday February 21st

I'm gonna be such a star. My Do Re Mis and wop-bop-a-loo-bops are going to be the envy of the toddling world. Excuse me whilst I go and practise – a-shooby-dooby-doo-wop a-shooby-doo-waa!!!!

Thursday February 22nd

You know, it's only a few days till my birthday, and I haven't noticed any mind-bogglingly elaborate preparations going on. The Oldies had better pull their fingers out before it's too late …

Friday February 23rd

Hmmm … This time last year they were booking clowns, buying in the jelly and ice-cream, sending out invites. The hustle and bustle was a joy to behold. This year there's not even a snifter of hustle, let alone any bustle. What's going on?

Saturday February 24th

Ah! I think I may have worked it out. It's going to be a surprise party! They are sweet. Ordinarily I'd have thought organising something like that was beyond them – Dad gets so excited that he normally gives the game away. But I must confess they've done a very good job of it so far. If I wasn't so intuitive, I wouldn't have a clue!

Sunday February 25th

Mum's just had a brand of shoes named after her! To be honest, I think 'Mum' is a pretty stupid name for a pair of shoes, but it's the thought that counts.

Still no sign of any birthday preparations.

They can't keep it a secret for ever – when are they going to put up the marquee?

Monday February 26th
I do hope Baby comes along to my surprise birthday party. I'll be the centre of events, and this time I won't be playing hard to get. She'll go weak at the knees when the birthday boy starts lavishing his attention upon her …

Tuesday February 27th
And Phoenix had better be there too. She's a bit of a know-all these days – it's about time she learned about real style …

Wednesday February 28th
I wonder if I'll get the chance to sing. A little light scatting perhaps wouldn't go amiss – a-shoop-wop a-diddlydiddly-dooo …

MARCH
2001

Thursday March 1st

Ooohhh!!!! Me poor ears. Spent the day practising my duet with Mum. I've got a nasty feeling our musical collaboration might be over before it's begun – musical differences, you understand. It's not that she isn't a fine musician, I just feel that artistically we're heading in different directions. Personally, I'd like to see us breaking new ground with what I like to call 'TOR' (that's Toddler-Orientated Rock) – kind of Mrs Madonna meets the

Krankees. Mum, on the other hand, seems determined to pursue her avant-garde 'Banshee with Laryngitis at Seven in the Morning after a Heavy Evening' sound, which, whilst undeniably distinctive, to be perfectly honest isn't my thing at all.

Ah well, I guess it's all part of the creative process. I'm happy to give Mum the benefit of my artistic prowess, but it's gonna have to be a one-off …

Friday March 2nd

I'm really getting rather excited. It's my big day on Sunday. Mum and Dad, bless 'em, are still keeping the secret with unprecedented brilliance. I'm rather hoping for my own recording studio for my birthday. I know Mum's got one, but really we both need our own space if we're not gonna get in each other's way both physically and artistically. Still, I'm not

going to make too much of a fuss about it –
as I approach the ripe old age of two I find
myself becoming a little less ambitious for
such transient goods and chattels. As long
as I have my family around me, I'm largely
content. They're a good laugh, if nothing
else …

Saturday March 3rd

This is rather an emotional day for me. A
day where I look back at the past two years
of my life, and consider my achievements.
All in all, life's been good to me. I've been
blessed with a set of parents who dote on
me like kids with a new toy – and I should
know, as I get new toys all the time. And
that, you see, is the nub of it. I know they're
a bit odd; I know they can be a bit
embarrassing; I know Dad looks like an
alien from time to time; but at the end of the
day, everything they do, they seem to do it

for yours truly. It's very sweet, really.

I almost feel guilty about all the secret time they've put into organising my surprise party for tomorrow. At least, I would if didn't know how much they enjoy it. I hope we're having jelly and ice-cream: it's one of Dad's favourites, and he deserves a bit of a treat.

Sunday March 4th

I DO NOT BLEEDIN' WELL BELIEVE IT!!!!!! After all the nice things I wrote about them yesterday! Party Schmarty – that couldn't have cost more than a couple of hundred nicker!

Easy, Brooklyn, easy. Let's not overreact, huh? You're two years old now, a dude of wisdom and experience. I take it all back – I can't deny that I had a pretty top-hole time. The Oldies did at least hire out my favourite joint for the occasion (a restaurant up the road where they lay a pretty mean spread and the strawberry milkshake is a gastronomic *tour de force*), and a few of my little chums came along – although Baby Spice and PC were conspicuous by their absence. I'm gonna have to speak to them about that …

All in all, though, it was a strangely humbling experience. Excuse me, my dear diary, if I'm getting a little reflective in my old age, but I wonder if it hasn't been good for me to have a birthday party that was a bit, well, ordinary. There is something strangely comforting about stepping outta the fast lane for a bit and acting like a normal kid. Even Mum and Dad were reasonably sensible – just enjoying the day without any celebrity, er, idiosyncrasies.

I rather feel I could get used to this. I've decided that this shall be my last entry. I know, I know, that's what I said on my first birthday, but then I was young and foolish. Now, in my new-found wisdom, I've decided to try and lead a normal life, and if I do that, then there's really going to be nothing to write about.

I just hope it rubs off on Mum and Dad …

Friday May 25th

HELP, HELP, HELP!!!! Diary, come to my arms. Aid me in my hour of need! At times like this, I need some way of giving vent to my feelings, and there's no point speaking to Mum and Dad – they've clearly finally flipped.

I thought Dad's hair was growing unusually long! But in my muddle-headed naïvety I reckoned it was just because he'd seen the light and wanted to look like everybody else. But no, daft old Brooklyn, I might have guessed he had an ulterior motive, a cunning plan to make himself look like a complete and utter 'nana.

So what's he done? He's only gawn and had a bleedin' mohican!!!!! This, my dear diary, takes the biscuit. In fact, it more than takes the biscuit, it takes the whole packet. No, actually, it takes the whole deluxe quality chocolate assortment tin. I don't know what he thinks he looks like, but he seems proud as peacock; in fact, that's just what he looks like – give him some brightly coloured feathers and he wouldn't look out of place in London Zoo.

But to be honest, dear diary, the fact that Dad's seen fit to make himself look like this opens up an altogether more serious can of worms. If he wants to do that to himself, well that's his decision – whatever bakes your cake, old bean. But let us not forget that when he went in for the boiled egg look, yours truly was inflicted with an identical haircut. Ordinarily I wouldn't even entertain the thought of them repeating the operation so that I look like my dear old daddio, but looking back at the crazy events of my world, I'm really not so sure.

Diary, excuse me. Time for me to make

myself scarce. I can hear Mum searching for the clippers. Oh my Gawd! I can hear footsteps – they're getting nearer. I'll keep you posted, but right now … I gotta hide!